SOCIAL WORK
WITH **TROUBLED**
FAMILIES

A CRITICAL INTRODUCTION

Edited by Keith Davies

Jessica Kingsley *Publishers*
London and Philadelphia

Bullet list on p.9 reproduced under the terms of the Open Government Licence v 3.0.
Bullet list on pp.104–5 reproduced under the terms of the Creative
Commons Attribution-ShareAlike 2.0 UK: England & Wales License.

First published in 2015
by Jessica Kingsley Publishers
73 Collier Street
London N1 9BE, UK
and
400 Market Street, Suite 400
Philadelphia, PA 19106, USA

www.jkp.com

Copyright © Jessica Kingsley Publishers 2015

Front cover image source: iStockphoto®.
The cover image is for illustrative purposes only.

Library of Congress Cataloging in Publication Data
Social work with troubled families : a critical introduction / edited by Keith Davies.
    pages cm
  ISBN 978-1-84905-549-9 (alk. paper)
  1. Family social work. 2. Dysfunctional families-
-Services for. I. Davies, Keith, 1955-
  HV697.S584 2015
  362.82'53--dc 3
                            2014037903

British Library Cataloguing in Publication Data
A CIP catalogue record for this book is available from the British Library

ISBN 978 1 84905 549 9
eISBN 978 0 85700 974 6

Printed and bound in the United States

CONTENTS

ACKNOWLEDGEMENTS 4

CHAPTER 1   Introducing the Troubled Families Programme. 5
Keith Davies, Kingston University

CHAPTER 2   Delivering Phase 1 of the Troubled Families
Programme: A Provider's Perspective 30
David Holmes CBE, Chief Executive, Family Action

CHAPTER 3   The Troubled Families Workforce and
Occupational Identity 53
Dr Sadie Parr, Sheffield Hallam University

CHAPTER 4   The 'Family Recovery' Approach to Helping
Struggling Families 74
Professor June Thoburn, University of East Anglia

CHAPTER 5   Troubled or Troublesome? Children Taken
into Care and Custody 100
*Carol Hayden and Craig Jenkins, Institute of Criminal
Justice Studies, University of Portsmouth*

CHAPTER 6   'Troubled Families': A Team Around the Family. . 124
*Ray Jones, Anna Matczak, Keith Davis and Ian Byford,
Kingston University and St George's, University of London*

CHAPTER 7   International Perspectives 159
Nigel Hall, Kingston University

CONTRIBUTORS 181

SUBJECT INDEX 184

AUTHOR INDEX 190

ACKNOWLEDGEMENTS

My thanks to the contributors for their scholarship, hard work and willingness to make time for this book amidst busy lives. Thanks too to Stephen and Danielle at Jessica Kingsley Publishers for their constant support. Finally, a particular thank you to my partner Suzanne, my sister Jude and my mother and father for their interest and love.

CHAPTER 1

Introducing the Troubled Families Programme

KEITH DAVIES, KINGSTON UNIVERSITY

Aims of the book

In December 2011, the Prime Minister launched a new programme to turn around the lives of 120,000 troubled families in England by 2015 (Department for Communities and Local Government (DCLG) 2012a, p.9).

This book aims to offer the reader a critical introduction to the Troubled Families Programme (TFP) and, although it does not provide a comprehensive analysis, it seeks to act as a sound starting point for more specialist studies and to refer those interested to further reading.

It is critical in that first it places the TFP in both policy and practice contexts, allowing the reader to form their own view regarding what is new in the approach, what is well founded and what might be problematic. Second, it benefits from the experience of those delivering services directly to families which, by virtue of this contact, carries a particular authenticity and expertise. Questions are raised regarding whole family work and indications for the development of future practice are formulated from the perspective of practice experience. Third, the findings of researchers are also strongly represented and the rigour of their practice provides a further authoritative perspective in what is a highly politicised and contested field. Finally, the TFP is placed in the context of international developments in whole family work, thus opening up more local thinking to the influence of different ideas. The book, therefore, attempts to provide a number of perspectives in the light of which the reader might work towards a personal understanding of the TFP.

The primary perspective from which the TFP is explored is that of professional practice and, primarily, social work practice. The initiative raises many urgent questions, for example concerning the best models of whole family work, the nature of the working relationship in social work and the ethics of assertive, intensive models of practice. Even more fundamentally, it questions whether troubled families work, in its directness and assertiveness, is social work at all and demands careful thinking about the appropriate training for Family Support Workers and the professional ethos under which they might best operate.

This is an opportune moment at which to consider an expanding, flagship social policy and to learn from the experience of initial implementation. In 2013, the National Audit Office (NAO) published an interim value-for-money evaluation of the TFP in which it noted significant successes whilst also voicing reservations regarding the ability of local authorities to identify the most needy families and the design of the Payment by Results (PBR) framework (DCLG 2012b, p.9). Considerable variation was noted between local authorities in their ability to 'attach' families to the programme, and the report emphasised the scope for learning from best practice. At the same time, it was announced in June 2013 that an extra £200 million would be made available to expand the TFP to include up to 400,000 families in 2015/16 and in the autumn budget of 2013 £40 million was committed to commence that expansion early in 2014/15. As the TFP agenda develops, this book sheds light on lessons from early implementation and comments on how the expansion might be designed in the light of contemporary evidence.

What is a troubled families intervention?

There is a good deal of diversity amongst interventions delivered under the TFP umbrella (National Audit Office 2013). However, they do have a common starting point in the practice framework for working with troubled families published by the DCLG (2012a), which identifies five core elements.

1. A dedicated worker, dedicated to a family

2. Practical 'hands on' support

3. A persistent, assertive and challenging approach

4. Considering the family as a whole – gathering the intelligence

5. Common purpose and agreed action

(DCLG 2012a, p.15)

Looking at these characteristics more closely, the centrality of a single worker engaging a family strongly is a hallmark of TFP interventions. Although the approach also tends to envisage a multi-professional 'team around the family', the foundations for subsequent work such as trust, engagement and motivation flow from the relationship between the key worker (often termed an Intensive Outreach Worker (IOW)) and the family. The word 'dedicated' is repeated in the bullet point above perhaps to emphasise the intensity of this role and the weight borne by the IOW's skills, values and qualities. They are not only dedicated in the sense of being allocated but also in that of being committed. Models can vary and, for example, Thoburn (2013) describes two key leads operating in a comparable Think Family project. There is also evidence of team members responding to families in the absence of the IOW (Thoburn 2013, p.232). However, the central role of the IOW is critical in the TFP and this arguably places the approach firmly in the relationship-based, social work tradition (Adams, Dominelli and Payne 2009; Howe 2009).

Another distinguishing quality of TFP interventions is the 'practical hands-on support' often undertaken by the IOW, which can take the form of housework, decoration, help with paperwork, support in preparing children for school in the mornings and the like. This approach reflects person-centred traditions in social work, which seek to locate work in those areas that are experienced by the service user as a priority (Adams *et al.* 2009; Howe 2009). At the same time, it draws on motivational and problem-solving theory (Howe 2009) in setting achievable and tangible goals early in contact to foster a sense of progress and, as a result, to consolidate engagement. This joining of the family in practical tasks is potentially powerful in terms of the working relationship through modelling and by countering any sense of distance, detached observation and judgement that the family might carry as an expectation of social work. Clearly, it also brings challenges regarding boundaries in the working relationship and defines social work in interesting ways in terms of role, task and location.

The style of TFP work is distinctive in being 'persistent, assertive and challenging' (DCLG 2012a, p.6). Referring to repeated visits and resilience in the face of reluctance, avoidance and even hostility, the term 'persistent' suggests a demonstration of commitment and determination on the part of staff. Of course, along with this use of power, ethical and human rights-based considerations arise. The need for careful thought about the boundaries between coercion and care becomes urgent. At the same time, questions arise for the way in which the working relationship is constructed. In this respect, Morris (2008, p.17) quotes Williams (2004) in drawing our attention to the principles of an ethic of care, the observation of which might act as a helpful guideline both of workers and families:

> These are the ethics which enable resilience, facilitate commitment and lie at the heart of people's interdependency. They constitute the compassionate realism of 'good enough' care. They include:
>
> - fairness
> - attentiveness to the needs of others
> - mutual respect
> - trust
> - reparation

- being non judgemental
- adaptability to new identities
- being prepared to be accommodating and
- being open to communication.

The guidance is clear (DCLG 2012a, p.25) that the TFP works on a 'whole family' basis recognising the interrelated nature of family experience. This should not mean working with several family members in parallel but, rather, generating a whole family assessment and plan. Ideally, this will allow work that is in tune with the unique 'rhythms' (DCLG 2012a, p.25) of individual families and that recognises and draws upon the resources and strengths located within them. Facilitating this is the multi-professional team around the family, configured in varied ways across different projects, supporting the central role of the IOW and affording what is often priority access to services. Members of this team may be staff with specialist skills in health, education, criminal justice, employment, housing and recovery from substance misuse. This model represents a response to the criticism that families with multiple needs have often received a fragmented and ineffective service from a range of services all working independently of each other.

The TFP has inherited a tradition from whole family approaches stretching back to the Dundee Family Project (Dillane 2001) of frankness with families regarding the consequences of non-participation. Straightforward discussion takes place of the likelihood of eviction, of a child becoming the subject of a Child Protection Plan or whatever the aversive action is that the family faces and has been related to referral. Following assessment, and in a similar spirit, a contract with goals is agreed under the auspices of the Troubled Families Co-ordinator and reviewed regularly with an expectation of change. Critics of this way of establishing 'common purpose' warn of coercion and of forcing disadvantaged families to take responsibility for social injustices that are not of their making (Gregg 2010). Proponents argue that honesty with families can cut across the drift, which does not help them (DCLG 2012a) and others point to the scope for creative social work provided by this sort of framework (Parr 2009) and to the often very positive outcomes reported by families (Jones *et al.* 2013; Parr 2009).

Who are troubled families?

To address this question in any depth, an explanation is needed of what is meant not only by 'troubled' but also 'family' and these terms are explored below. However, at this point, a more pragmatic approach is adopted by simply considering the characteristics of families included in the TFP. The DCLG (2012a, p.9) defines troubled families eligible for the TFP as:

> those who meet 3 of the 4 following criteria:
>
> • Are involved in youth crime or anti-social behaviour
>
> • Have children who are regularly truanting or not in school
>
> • Have an adult on out of work benefits
>
> • Cause high costs to the taxpayer.

The document goes on to define more closely what is meant by each criterion.

In its guidance to local authorities in selecting their proportion of the 120,000 families participating in the programme nationally, the DCLG (2012b) advises that any family meeting all of the first three criteria should be regarded as a troubled family and included in the programme. Where a family meets two of the first three criteria, the fourth 'filter' criterion is to be applied using local discretion and might serve to include families with a child subject to a Child Protection Plan for example, families to whom police are frequently called out or those who experience health difficulties.

The DCLG guidelines also anticipate that many families will experience a much wider range of challenges than those indicated by the main criteria above and are supported in this by the findings of research studies (Hayden and Jenkins 2013; Jones *et al.* 2013; Thoburn *et al.* 2013). Turning very briefly to recent research, it indicates that, in terms of demographics, participating families vary in race and ethnicity according to the location of the studies but tend to demonstrate a higher proportion of single parent families than the national average, larger families and ones with lower income (see below for a discussion of the complexity of defining family membership and 'practice' (Morris 2008, 2013)). Regarding family problems, the consistent prevalence of ill-health – both physical and mental – is noteworthy (Boddy *et al.* 2012; Gregg 2010), as are domestic violence, debt, housing-related concerns and substance misuse (Hayden and Jenkins 2013; Morris 2013; Thoburn *et al.* 2013). Academics and researchers reporting the family interventions that immediately preceded the TFP also found a similar set of family characteristics and problems (Dillane *et al.* 2001; Lloyd *et al.* 2011; Morris *et al.* 2008; Nixon, Parr and Hunter 2008; Parr 2009; Thoburn 2010; White *et al.* 2008).

Whilst listing family patterns and circumstances is informative, it can also obscure the interaction between sets of problems and the impact of both cumulative and interrelated problems in a family's experience. At the same time, the attention to 'trouble' can obscure the strengths that families show, the resources and resilience they generate and the ways of coping that they create and recreate in the face of change. The literature relating to the TFP highlights the dynamic and interrelated nature of the challenges faced by families that we might think of as troubled (Casey 2012; Hayden and Jenkins 2013) and the approach itself reflects this in its 'whole family' and multi-professional aspects. It is also rich in case studies and in the voices of service users (Casey 2012; DCLG 2012a) and this can help to communicate the resilience demonstrated by families as well as the despair. It should be noted that a fine ethical sensitivity is needed in representing the voices of families if patronisation is to be avoided. Vigilance is also required in resisting any temptation to exaggerate either the difficulties which families face or the successes which they achieve.

It is important, when exploring the commonalities amongst families involved in TFP-style initiatives, not to lose sight of their diversity. Morris (2008, p.18) draws attention to the need to understand families that are marginalised in a number of ways and discusses Black and Minority Ethnic families in particular.

Why a troubled families programme?

Amongst the reasons supporting the £448 million investment from the inception of the TFP in 2012 to 2015, the question of public expenditure is prominent. The DCLG (2012b) estimates that the cost to the taxpayer of providing services to families in difficulty is £9 billion per year or £75,000 per family, with the vast majority of that sum (£8 billion) taken up in reactive measures such as accommodating children and funding Pupil Referral Units. Viewing this as a perennial and ineffective expense whilst, at the same time, seeking to reduce public expenditure, the Coalition Government launched the TFP with a view to resolving ongoing family difficulties and their associated costs. The language of 'turning around' is in line with this financial goal and reflects the belief that families will be transformed, or at least returned to a normative level of cost to the state, on a permanent basis.

The figure of 120,000 derives in part from calculations made in 2005 of the number of families experiencing multiple social disadvantages. It is contested and Levitas (2012, p.4) provides a detailed and critical analysis. More recently, it has been announced (DCLG 2013) that the TFP is to be extended in 2015/16 to encompass 400,000 families, casting doubt, perhaps, on the original definition. Despite these variations in numbers, however, the thinking persists that a relatively small proportion of families are responsible for disproportionate claims on the public purse. In responding to this, it is estimated that a TFP intervention will cost up to £10,000 per family, of which central government will provide £4,000 (Wincup 2013) and local authorities the remainder. The £4,000 central government contribution is made up of an initial start-up or 'attachment' element with a second instalment available on a PBR basis, where programme outcomes are met (DCLG 2012b). Concerns have been expressed that the published PBR criteria fail to reflect 'the complex health, wellbeing and relationship problems' with which families in need tend to struggle alongside the meeting of their children's needs (Thoburn forthcoming). The emphasis on employment and anti-social behaviour (ASB) in the PBR formula may tend to exclude families with other pressing needs and the ways in which TFP work is incentivised represents an important issue for future development.

Turning to ASB, it represents a further thread in the rationale underpinning the TFP, founded on the perception that some families cause a disproportionate amount of nuisance and distress for their neighbours and community. As we see below, this thinking has long roots (Parr 2009) and was reflected in the 'Respect Agenda' of the New Labour Government (Respect Task Force 2006). However, commentators (Hayden and Jenkins 2013) have also noted the influence of the disturbances or riots of August 2011 on the TFP and this element of the rationale remains influential.

A third aspect of the rationale for the TFP might seem somewhat at odds with these concerns about cost and ASB. However, commentators (Hayden and Jenkins 2013; Parr 2009) have consistently pointed out that motivations for the initiative seem mixed and the thinking behind it hybrid. The DCLG (2012a, p.9), states that: 'Troubled families are those that have problems and often cause problems'.

In a speech on troubled families made in 2011, David Cameron said that: 'people in troubled families aren't worthless or pre-programmed to fail' and, with reference to the TFP, he went on to claim that:

> we will be human: engaging with families as the messy, varied, living, breathing groups of different people they actually are... The message is this: 'we are not coming in to rescue you – you need to rescue yourselves, but we will support you every step of the way.' (Cameron 2011)

Although the TFP is certainly not a traditional welfare initiative, it is, nevertheless, possible to detect welfare qualities albeit sea changed by a new politics. The announcement here is of a supportive, state-funded programme targeted at least in part on need, and the methods of delivery, as we shall soon see, are at least in part recognisable as relationship-based, psychosocial social work.

There are, therefore, at least three inter-related reasons in the official literature for the establishment of the TFP including a drive to save costs, a desire to reduce ASB (and to be seen to be responding robustly to it) and a 'tough-love' approach to need and distress.

Terminology

In creating a context for the chapters that follow, it will be important to examine the language in which the TFP and the discussion related to it is couched. Words such as 'troubled', 'turned around' and even 'family' have a common-sense meaning that is apparently straightforward, and attempts to examine language can be represented as irrelevant and obstructive to action. However, as has been realised powerfully in the field of equality and diversity, values and theory are always embedded in 'common sense' (Thompson 2012) and in everyday language. As we use the discourse of 'troubled families', it constructs our perceptions in certain ways (for example, by locating the trouble in the family) and creates subjects such as the troubled family itself, the 'trouble shooter' as the IOW is sometimes known, and the state of being turned around, which are then considered to be real, concrete phenomena shaping decisions and experiences. Therefore, it is important to think carefully and responsibly about language and the understandings it creates.

The term 'troubled family' is supported by studies of those involved in Family Intervention Projects (FIPs) and TFP-type interventions (Casey 2012; Morris 2008; Nixon *et al.* 2008; Thoburn 2010) in as much as they report a wide range of troubles such as ill health, low income and poor housing as typically experienced by participating families (see the 'Who are troubled families?' section above). As a signifier of stress and need, the term seems to correspond with experience. However, the identification of 120,000 such families implies a very clear distinction between families that are troubled and those that are not when it might be argued that most families, at one point or another, are troubled. The danger here is that of creating a stigmatised or 'othered' group existing as a 'them' to everyone else's 'us,' and this is borne out by some of the journalistic reports of the TFP (Woodhouse 2014).

It will be important to bear this difficulty in mind, particularly when it is hoped that families will not be discouraged from engaging with the TFP by its title and reputation and will not internalise a sense of themselves through it as being of low worth and unlikely to change.

Commentators (Garrett 2009; Levitas 2012) have pointed out a second danger concerning the word troubled. To the extent that the TFP represents a response to ASB, it appears to address troublesome rather than troubled families (Wincup 2013). This changes the grammar of the debate as neighbours and communities replace families as the subject of the TFP and families become the object of interventions designed to stop the trouble they cause. In social policy terms, this would be much more of a controlling project than a welfare one.

Third, as noted above, the language of troubled families has been interpreted as implying that families themselves are the source of their own woes and that the onus is on them to change their unhelpful behaviours. In response, Garret (2009), Gregg (2010) and Levitas (2012) amongst others have objected to the way in which this ignores the impact of economic disadvantage on families and shifts the blame from unjust social relations onto individuals. Others add that the language of trouble discounts the resources, strengths and resilience that families demonstrate in the face of adversity (Morris 2008; Wincup 2013).

There have been numerous attempts at alternative terminology. Placing the emphasis on structural dynamics, Levitas (2012, p.12) uses the term 'families experiencing multiple disadvantages' whilst Morris (2008, p.6) speaks of 'families enduring multiple and chronic difficulties' (p.13). Perhaps seeking to avoid stigma and labelling, providers have also sought alternative language for their troubled families' interventions, preferring 'Family Recovery Project' and 'Strengthening Families' amongst other titles. In recognition of family strengths as well as problems, the Family Rights Group has referred to 'struggling families' evoking the language of political protest as well as of travail.

The term 'family' is clearly embedded at the heart of language about the TFP and describes such a fundamental, everyday social unit that its meaning can easily be taken for granted as self-evident. However, as Wincup (2013) and Morris (2008, 2013) remind us, the structures, membership and day-to-day ways of living of families are extremely diverse. Ethnic and cultural considerations are influential in creating family diversity, as is class although there are also wide differences between families that share cultural or class identity (Wincup 2013). In addition, it is well documented that broad patterns of family composition and role change significantly over time (Morris 2008; Williams 2004; Wincup 2013). As Morris (2008) cautions, there is a danger that politically driven, normative and romanticised conceptions of what a family is can undermine effective practice with real families that are constituted and function very differently. Practitioners, as well as policy makers, can undermine practice by perceiving negatively those families that fail to reflect the unexamined and rather fixed norms they carry with them. As Morris (2013, p.201) observes, 'The term family is used indiscriminately in much of the relevant policy and practice literature emerging over the past decade, with various implicit assumptions about meanings.'

As Morris (2008) also notes, notions of what a family should be tend to revolve around relations of kinship, cohabitation in a shared space and patterns of care giving, particularly childcare. However, in support of more nuanced ways of understanding families, she suggests that family definition is something that families themselves do best (2008, 2013). That is, rather than applying an external, theoretical image of family structure and roles, policy makers and practitioners might instead listen to families as they describe who they are. In the same spirit, Morris (2008, 2013) and Parr (2009) draw our attention to individual 'family practices' and to the 'lived experience' of particular families. Following their advice, we might pay attention to the idiosyncratic and detailed ways of living within a family and how it views the world (including Social Workers and other professionals) at the heart of our understanding. In doing so, we might adopt a more 'functional' and less 'normative' definition of family (Morris 2008, p.15).

The aim of the TFP is to 'turn around' troubled families, suggesting a sustainable, transformative, 180-degree shift in attitudes, behaviours and direction. The language is dynamic and radical ascribing an active role to those intervening and placing the locus of change firmly in families rather than in the environment around them. A narrative of personal responsibility and of muscular, effective government is woven into the language, which, it should be borne in mind, is designed for a political arena. However, research studies do reflect an experience of positive change characterised by some families as transformative (Jones *et al.* 2013; Parr 2009) and it is, perhaps, unsurprising that intense, well-resourced and highly relational social work can result in a unique shift for some.

Interviews with both service users and stakeholders provided compelling evidence to suggest that the intervention provided by Signpost (a family intervention project guided by a professional ethos founded in social work) was pivotal in helping families make, sometimes remarkable, transformations (Parr 2009, p.1264).

For others, the effects, although valuable, may be less dramatic and, indeed, the criteria for PBR suggest that change short of total family renewal can be regarded as a 'turning around'. Keeping a sense of perspective about the language of change and valuing interim, transitional shifts seems sensible whilst at the same time retaining the belief that families can and, in the right circumstances sometimes do, transform themselves.

The policy context

The reader will already have sensed that the TFP and its predecessors are, as Parr (2009) describes, composite in terms of the values and thinking that underpin them. Considering FIPs, she observes that:

> critical analysis of this ever-evolving policy agenda indicates that it does not coalesce around a coherent theoretical framework but is a hybrid of punitive, responsibilizing and remoralizing sentiments built on a mixed bag of understandings, ideologies and concepts, many of which have been influenced by ideas and practices from the USA. (Parr 2009, p.1257)

Hayden and Jenkins (2013, p.10) concur, referring to the TFP as reflecting 'a confusing agenda' and Boddy *et al.* (2012, pp.8–9) call for 'an explicit theoretical base for intensive family intervention'.

In very broad terms, the TFP might be said on the one hand to embody welfare policy by deploying centrally allocated resources to fund intensive support to meet severe need through social work services. Indeed, for all the concern about the criminalisation of social policy, Parr (2009) notes something of a reverse process on the ground as policy is 'socialized' (p.1270) by delivery through interpersonal means informed by social work values. However, on the other hand, the focus on family behaviours, the preoccupation with cost saving and the intrusive, persistent, sanctions-related features of the initiative speak more of a neo-liberal social policy agenda (Simpson and Connor 2011). This makes for tensions within the policy and goes some way towards explaining how varied and how strongly held the interpretations of it have been (DCLG 2012; Gregg 2010).

Those adopting a critical approach have, perhaps, given most attention to the historical development of policy, although Thoburn (forthcoming) traces the formative influence of the Family Service Units and their style of intensive, empathic psychosocial family work on the FIPs and subsequently the TFP. Garrett (2009), for example, refers to Macnicol's (1987) work on the construction of an '"undeserving" segment of the population in the late nineteenth century' (Garrett 2009, p.103) arguing that the state characteristically deflects responsibility for the effects of structural oppression from itself by locating the problem instead in the attitudes and behaviours of 'indisciplined' families. In the same vein, Welshman (2011) traces a genealogy of the 'underclass' from ideas of the 'social residuum' in the late nineteenth century to the present day arguing that, 'in the modern period, since c.1880, there have been at least eight major reconstructions.' In the 1880s, social investigators such as Charles Booth became concerned about the emergence of a 'social residuum' in London. This was echoed by anxieties about the 'unemployable' in the writings of William Beveridge and the social reformers Beatrice and Sidney Webb in the early 1900s.

He goes on to trace the 'reconstructions' of the problematic family motif through the 'problem family' emerging as a concept in the Second World War, via Sir Keith's Joseph's popularisation of ideas of 'cycles of deprivation' within families in the 1970s, the notion of 'the underclass' proper deriving from Murray in the 1990s (Murray 1990) through to concerns about social exclusion under New Labour. In particular, Welshman (2012, p.104) draws attention to the 1943 publication by the National Federation of Women's Institutions of Our Towns, a report on the state of urban families following experiences of evacuation. The report identified a 'submerged tenth', which included 'problem families' whom it reported as often associated with chronic poverty, crime, ASB, mental and physical ill-health, the neglect of children and nuisance to others. Indeed, Starkey (2000), traces links between the concept of the problem family in the 1940s and eugenicist thinking. Without wishing to suggest any association between the TFP and eugenics, its focus on families' functioning, characterisation of them as problematic for society and attempt to quantify their prevalence all bear a resemblance to past approaches to families deemed problematic. In this way, critical voices helpfully draw attention to the impact on families of poverty and warn against abuse of the power to intervene in homes and family lives.

More recent policy development is described by White *et al.* (2008), who note that it was initially associated closely with responses to ASB under the New Labour Government.

Combating ASB has been of political interest since the late 1990s but became a priority concern for the Government in 2002. In 2003 the ASB Act was introduced, the Home Office's Anti-Social Behaviour Unit (ASBU) was established (October 2003) and the ASB 'Together' Action Plan was launched.

Work relating to ASB adopted an enforcement approach, for example around Anti-Social Behaviour Orders but, in turn, drew attention to families with severe and combined problems. As a result of this, White *et al.* (2008, p.10) note that, 'it also became evident that a combined approach of enforcement and support was required to address the deep seated underlying problems of these families in order to reduce their ASB.'

A number of intensive family support projects were piloted based on the reported success of the Dundee Family Project (Dillane *et al.* 2001) and, in 2006, the Respect Task Force under

The Respect Action Plan was given responsibility for the development of 50 Intensive FIPs across the country. The policy focus had thus moved from a narrower focus on the control of ASB itself towards its deeper causes and, in particular, towards those causes located in families.

The Coalition Government inherited this policy thread in 2010 and has largely retained it. Some further changes of tack can be discerned in the new emphasis through the fiscal case and PBR on reductions in public spending, but it might be argued that the Troubled Families Team set up under the Department for Communities and Local Government (DCLG) in 2012 and the launch of the TFP represent a good deal of continuity with previous policy.

The practice context

At its launch the TFP was represented as a new initiative, and certainly aspects such as PBR and the target of turning around 120,000 families were indeed new. However, as has been noted, there were also substantial continuities in the service user group targeted and in the style of intervention between the TFP and its immediate predecessors, the FIPs. Indeed, the history of social work interventions in the lives of families facing multiple challenges has been relatively long.

Payne (2005, p.36), when discussing the origins of social work, refers to 'a method of "friendly visiting" evolved from the work of Octavia Hill in the London housing movement, where female visitors would assist women in organising and planning their family life and budgets more effectively.'

Although this is not 'whole family' work as defined here, it does indicate a tradition, as far back as the nineteenth century, of identifying families whose functioning is deemed problematic and of working for change in the setting of the family home. The work of the Family Service Units after the Second World War is also relevant and has been mentioned above (Starkey 2000; Thoburn forthcoming). Thoburn (2013, p.228) also notes that, 'the long tradition in the UK and USA of whole family approaches to service provision for families with complex problems is documented in the policy, research and social work practice literature'.

She herself points to family preservation models such as the Home Builders approach practised in the later years of the last century, which worked through the intensive availability of an experienced Social Worker for short periods (Frazer, Nelson and Rivard 1997).

However, in terms of the TFP's immediate predecessors, it is accepted both by the Government (DCLG 2012a) and by researchers (Gregg 2010; Lloyd *et al.* 2011; Parr 2009) that the Dundee Family Project (Dillane *et al.* 2001) pioneered the approaches essential to troubled family interventions and formed a prototype for them. Located primarily in housing, this project sought to intervene in the lives of families that were either homeless or at risk of homelessness through rent arrears and ASB. Using a core residential unit to house some homeless families, dispersed and supported accommodation for others and a third outreach element where families had not yet been evicted, the model was intensive and oriented towards the whole family.

The project followed a systemic approach to family difficulties and offered a range of services through individual and couple counselling, family support and group work. The service made support available 24 hours a day, all year. Staff ran after-school and young persons' group activities, while groups for adults covered cookery, parenting skills, anger management and tenancy issues (Dillane *et al.* 2001, p.vi).

Practice methods were 'premised on a systematic, holistic assessment process and joint "contracting" about what is to be done' (Dillane *et al.* 2001, p.17). They were also 'intensive...time-limited...and focused very clearly on the goals' (p.17) In total, 59 per cent of family outcomes were judged to be successful when either all the goals set or at least the main ones were achieved. However, the authors note that, 'the information in the records on outcomes varied in specificity, so it was only possible to make crude categorisations based on this' (p.43).

The six subsequent pilot projects in the north of England (DCLG 2006; Lloyd *et al.* 2011; Respect Task Force 2006) adopted a similar practice framework and DCLG (2006) report that complaints of ASB against 85 per cent of participating families effectively ceased whilst the tenancies of 80 per cent were secured and project workers assessed that in 92 per cent of families the threat to local communities had reduced.

As outlined above, FIPs came into being under the Respect Action Plan and embodied a significant expansion in family interventions. Lloyd et al. (2011, p.3) provide a detailed evaluation of these projects but summarise broadly thus.

In total, 3675 families exited a family intervention between February 2007 and 31 March 2011:

- Seventy per cent (2569 families) left for a successful reason.

- Four per cent (142 families) left for an unsuccessful reason.

- Nine per cent (316 families) left for an inconclusive reason (i.e. a reason that could not be counted as successful or unsuccessful).

- Eighteen per cent (648 families) were recorded as having both successful and unsuccessful reasons for leaving, or no reason for leaving was given.

Although the succession of favourable research findings is strong, Gregg (2010), in a powerful critique, takes issue with the methodology on which they are based. Pointing to, amongst a range of concerns, a lack of control groups and relatively small samples, he questions their validity. At the same time, he suggests that findings are 'talked up' by politicians, who ignore the scholarly caveats and warnings of limitations included by researchers.

The DCLG (2012a, see p.11 and pp.34–35) acknowledges some of these criticisms, mentioning specifically the absence of control groups, small samples and the use of practitioners' judgements in establishing success in some cases. Correspondingly, it is noted that, 'this means that this evidence, of course, should not be taken as representative of all troubled families' (DCLG 2012a, p.11).

However, it concludes that:

The main strength of the evidence base is the consistency of findings over a number of different evaluations, as well as the consistency in monitoring outcomes reported in the national monitoring reports. Published research evaluating family intervention projects have all reported largely positive results in terms of outcomes for families, cost-efficiency, and approval from service users. (p.34)

The Troubled Families Programme and professional practice

There is evidence that existing service provision finds 'thinking family' both challenging and controversial, and this has implications for professional knowledge and frameworks, training and ultimately the arrival at shared objectives (Morris 2008, p.6).

In creating a context for the discussions that follow, brief consideration will be given to the questions, challenges and stimuli that the TFP model of whole family practice poses for professional practice and, in particular, for social work.

Looking first at practice methods, Morris (2008) notes that whole family approaches are in the relatively early stages of their development. Whilst there are related practice strands across a wide range of service user groups, the theory base is in the early days of development. Fundamental questions such as which families might benefit from this approach and which might not await answers and the role of service users in the development of theory and practice also require urgent attention.

There are clear links between TFP-style interventions and more established practice approaches such as Crisis Intervention, Ecological Systems Theory, Person-centred Practice, Systemic Family Therapy and also with theory relating to Inter-professional Practice. An exciting task exists of tracing the relationship between whole family approaches and these theoretical and practice traditions.

In developing theory for whole family work, the question of responsiveness to diversity is urgent, as is a related question concerning the degree to which it would be helpful to codify and unify practices rather than, as Morris (2008, p.71) and

Thoburn (2013) suggest, retaining a degree of flexibility around key principles.

We concur with Flint (2011, p.131) that:

> Rather than attempting to identify one project or model of delivery that is most effective there is a need to recognise that a range of initiatives and approaches are required to achieve positive outcomes with a diverse range of young people and families. However, holistic whole family approaches, multi-agency partnerships, a key worker, intensity and longevity of engagement and access to specialist and statutory support services will be common elements of successful approaches. (Thoburn 2013, p.235)

A further set of questions concerns arrangements for service delivery. At present, a range of providers located both in the voluntary and statutory sectors offer TFP interventions. The duration of intervention varies, as does the configuration of teams and roles. Some commentators have argued for the importance of the provider embracing and expressing a 'social work ethos' (Parr 2009; Thoburn 2013) but the effects of different organisational culture and contrasting modes of delivery await detailed exploration.

It will be clear from what has been said already that the style of the TFP model challenges traditional professional practices in a number of ways. First, there are the challenges presented by assertive practice. Casey (2012, p.4) emphasises, 'the use of persistence and assertiveness with families to keep them engaged and following agreed steps.' (Hayden and Jenkins 2013).

Indeed, the DCLG describes services users finding TFP staff, 'bolshy', 'nagging', 'challenging', and 'forceful.' (DCLG 2012a, p.23).

How far is this relational style and use of power compatible with professional values of respect and the principle of autonomy? Is there a model here for practice more widely, which, it might be implied, has historically been unhelpfully unassertive? Alongside these questions are others arising from the intensity and location of TFP practice. Practitioners can find that the TFP milieu gives them a freedom from tight administrative requirements, a degree of discretion, a freedom from office-based practice environments and the sort of time with service users that can be rare in other settings (Parr 2009, p.1257). However, with the intimacy and strength of this sort of often home-based contact come important questions regarding boundaries in the working relationship, the management of potential dependency and the conduct of endings or processes of stepping down. As Thoburn (forthcoming, p.3) asks, to what extent should there be gradations of intensity of TFP intervention both at the initial referral stage (especially as 400,000 families are now to participate, not all of whom might be suited to the most intense model) and in the course of the work as families work towards exiting the programme?

Finally, as Hayden and Jenkins (2013, p.10) found, 'many professionals believed that "who works" is at least as important as the programmatic approaches, or "what works"'.

Being so intensely relational, the TFP model lends urgency to questions about which qualities, values, knowledge and skills are required of family support staff. This question, in turn, has implications for the status, remuneration, recruitment and training of Family Intervention Workers.

The last of the challenges for professional practice deriving from the TFP to be mentioned here concerns the relationship between TFP work and mainstream service provision. Despite the planned expansion of the TFP, it will nevertheless be available for only a minority of families. The relationship between whole family work and other services requires careful consideration. There may be concern that the TFP attracts priority access to resources and the potential for splitting is clear where responsibility for safeguarding is retained by a children's services Social Worker whose contact with the family follows a very different pattern from that adopted by the TFP. This requires careful management and Thoburn (forthcoming, p.8) warns of the 'insulation' of whole family units from children's and adult's safeguarding. The separate organisation of children's and adults' services creates potential barriers to whole family work.

The structure of the book

This introduction has attempted to map out a context in which the subsequent chapters, which form the essential body of the book, can be placed. For the reader approaching the field for the first time or with a brief acquaintance with the TFP, it may be helpful to read this chapter first.

The body of the book reflects three important perspectives on the TFP. In Chapters 2 and 3, service providers in both the voluntary and statutory sectors reflect on their experience and suggest ways in which the TFP might change and develop. Important points, illustrated through case studies, are made regarding the criteria for family inclusion, the structure of the PBR framework, the design of the commissioning framework, the nature of the challenges faced by families and models of practice intervention.

Chapters 4, 5, 6 and 7 are founded on research studies related either to the TFP itself or to its immediate predecessors, the FIPs and Think Family pilot studies. In Chapter 4, Parr's careful description of two FIPs based on contrasting professional traditions and cultures allows her to ask key questions about the professional ethos on which the TFP should be founded, the nature of the training required by practitioners and the remuneration offered to them. Echoing some of these concerns and introducing others in Chapter 4, Thoburn reflects on a multi-agency Think Family intervention in the light of an ethnographic study. Offering evidence for the value of an inter-professional model located in statutory children's services, she is able to highlight neglected areas of family need such as mental health and disability whilst drawing attention to the importance of practitioners' relational, advocacy and mediation skills. In Chapter 5, Hayden and Jenkins tease out the relationship between troubled and troublesome families through a detailed report on the study of children in one local authority, on the one hand, taken into care ('troubled') and on the other taken into custody ('troublesome'). At the same time as raising specific questions, for example about data sharing protocols in multi-professional contexts, they also raise wider ones regarding the impact of relative poverty on families and the relevance of the broader structural context to the TFP. Finally, in this research-based series, in Chapter 6 Jones and colleagues bring the views of service users and related agencies through a report on the findings of a qualitative study of their experiences of a contemporary troubled families project. Shedding light on family responses to the style of intervention, they also raise questions regarding the sustainability of family changes.

Chapter 7 is the last of the substantive chapters and in it Hall makes a contrasting contribution by looking towards international work with families with complex and interrelated challenges. In so doing, he adds a dimension to the potential learning about this sort of work as it develops and helps to prevent the narrowness of thought that might characterise a wholly local debate. Drawing on work in a wide range of work across continents, this chapter supports reflection on what we mean by a family, on the relationship between family and community and on the imaginative responses developed where trouble is often startlingly intense and resources alarmingly sparse. Drawing attention to initiatives in community capacity building and reciprocal exchange alongside more radical structural change, international practice offers fresh possibilities to more local thinking.

The book concludes by reflecting briefly on the indications for future policy and practice presented in the preceding chapters.

References

Adams, R., Dominelli, L. and Payne, M. (eds) (2009) *Social Work: Themes, Issues and Critical Debates.* Basingstoke: Palgrave Macmillan.

Boddy, J., Statham, J., Warwick, I., Hollingworth, K. and Spencer, G. (2012) *Health Related Work in Family Intervention Projects.* London: Thomas Coram Research Unit.

Cameron, D. (2005) *Troubled Families Speech.* London: Cabinet Office and Prime Minister's Office. Available at www.gov.uk/government/speeches/troubled-families-speech, accessed on 11 October 2014.

Casey, L. (2012) *Listening to Troubled Families.* London: DCLG.

Department for Communities and Local Government (2006) *Anti-social Behaviour Intensive Family Support Projects.* Housing Research Summary 230. London: DCLG.

Department for Communities and Local Government (2012a) *Working with Troubled Families: A Guide to the Evidence and Good Practice.* London: DCLG.

Department for Communities and Local Government (2012b) *The Troubled Families Programme: Financial Framework for the Troubled Families Programme's Payment-by-results Scheme for Local Authorities.* London: DCLG.

Dillane, J., Hill, M., Bannister, J. and Scott, S. (2001) *Evaluation of the Dundee Families Project.* Edinburgh: The Stationery Office.

Flint, J. (2011) *Evaluation of Rochdale Families Project: Policy Contexts and Research Evidence.* Sheffield: Sheffield Hallam University, Centre for Regional Economic and Social Research.

Frazer, M.W., Nelson, C.E. and Rivard, J.C. (1997) 'Effectiveness of Family Services.' *Social Work Research 21,* 3, 138–53.

Garrett, P. (2009) '*Transforming' Children's Services: Social Work, Neoliberalism and the 'Modern' World.* Maidenhead: The Open University Press.

Gregg, D. (2010) *Family Intervention Projects: A Classic Case of Policy-based Evidence.* London: Kings College, Centre for Crime and Justice Studies.

Hayden, C. and Jenkins, C. (2013) 'Children taken into care and custody and the "troubled families" agenda in England.' *Child and Family Social Work.* Available at http://onlinelibrary.wiley.com/doi/10.1111/cfs.12095/abstract, accessed on 11 October 2014.

HM Treasury, the Rt Hon Danny Alexander MP, The Rt Hon EHC Pickles MP and Department for Communities and Local Government (2013) Massive expansion of Troubled Families programme announced. Available at www.gov.uk/government/news/massive-expansion-of-troubled-families-programme-announced, accessed on 8 November 2014.

Howe, D. (2009) *A Brief Introduction to Social Work Theory.* Basingstoke: Palgrave Macmillan.

Jones, R., Matczak, A., Byford, I. and Davies, K. (2013) *Wandsworth Family Recovery Project: Views of Families and Other Agencies.* Kingston-upon-Thames: Kingston University.

Levitas, R. (2012) 'There may be "trouble" ahead: what we know about those 120,000 "troubled" families.' *Poverty and Social Exclusion in the UK.* Policy Response Series No. 3. Swindon: ESCRC.

Lloyd, C., Wollney, I., White, C. and Purdon, S. (2011) *Monitoring and Evaluation of Family Intervention Services and Projects Between Feb 2007 and March 2011.* Research Report DFE-RR 174. London: The Department for Education.

Macnicol, J. (1987) 'In pursuit of the underclass.' *Journal of Social Policy 16,* 3, 293–318.

Morris, K., Hughes, N., Clarke, H., Tew, J., Mason, P., Galvani, S., Lewis, A. and Loveless, L. (2008) *Think Family: A Literature Review of Whole Family Approaches.* London: Cabinet Office, Social Exclusion Task Force.

Morris, K. (2013) 'Troubled families: vulnerable families' experiences of multiple service use.' *Child and Family Social Work 18,* 198–206.

Murray, C. (1990) *The Emerging British Underclass.* London: The Institute of Economic Affairs.

National Audit Office (2013) *Programmes to Help Families Facing Multiple Challenges.* London: National Audit Office.

Nixon, J., Parr, S. and Hunter, C. (2008) *The Longer-term Outcomes Associated with Families who had Worked with Intensive Family Support Projects.* London: DCLG.

Parr, S. (2009) 'Family Intervention Projects: A site of social work practice.' *British Journal of Social Work 39,* 1256–1273.

Payne, M. (2005) *The Origins of Social Work: Continuity and Change.* Basingstoke: Palgrave Macmillan.

Simpson, G. and Connor, S. (2011) *Social Policy for Social Welfare Professionals: Tools for Understanding, Analysis and Engagement.* Bristol: The Policy Press.

Starkey, P. (2000) *Families and Social Workers: The Work of Family Service Units 1940–1985.* Liverpool: Liverpool University Press.

Respect Task Force (2006) *Respect Action Plan.* London: Home Office.

Thoburn, J. (2010) 'Towards knowledge-based practice in complex child protection cases: a research-based expert briefing.' *Journal of Children's Services 5,* 1, 9–24.

Thoburn, J., Cooper, N., Brandon, M. and Connolly, S. (2013) 'The place of "think family" approaches in child and family social work: Messages from a process evaluation of an English pathfinder service.' *Children and Youth Services Review 35,* 228–236.

Thoburn, J. (forthcoming) *Families, Relationships and Societies: 'Troubled Families', 'Troublesome Families' and the Trouble with Payment by Results.*

Thompson, N. (2012) *Anti-discriminatory Practice* (5th edition). Basingstoke: Macmillan.

Welshman, J. (2011) *'Troubled Families': The Lessons of History, 1880–2012.* London: History and Policy. Available at www.historyandpolicy.org/papers/policy-paper-136.html#S1, accessed on 11 October 2014.

White, C., Warrener, M., Reeves, A. and La Valle, I. (2008) *Family Intervention Projects: An Evaluation of their Design, Set-up and Early Outcomes.* London: National Centre for Social Research.

Wincup, E. (2013) *Understanding Crime and Social Policy.* Bristol: Policy Press.

Williams, F. (2004) *Rethinking Families.* London: Calouste Gulbenkian Foundation.

Woodhouse, C. (2014) 'Tiny tearaways will be targeted by "Shameless squads".' *The Sun* 23 March 2014.

CHAPTER 2

Delivering Phase 1 of the Troubled Families Programme

A Provider's Perspective

DAVID HOLMES CBE, CHIEF EXECUTIVE, FAMILY ACTION

Introduction

Family Action has been a leading family support charity since its origins in 1869. It is particularly well known for its intensive work with families in their own homes and for its success in working with families with multiple and complex needs. As such, it was a natural fit as a potential provider of the Troubled Families Programme (TFP). To date, Family Action has been commissioned by seven local authorities across England to provide Troubled Families services under Phase 1 of the TFP. In this chapter I reflect on our experience of delivering Phase 1 of the TFP in different parts of England and the successes and the challenges that we have encountered along the way. I also suggest how that delivery experience might help to inform Phase 2, given the welcome news that the TFP is to be extended into the next Parliament.

Family Action is a strong supporter of the TFP. The charity's mission is to 'preserve and protect the good health (in particular mental health) of families, individuals and groups within the community and the relief of poverty' so how could we not support the TFP? In our experience of family intervention, the TFP is exactly right in seeking to join up local services and agencies, in having a whole family approach, in promoting a model of working in which a key worker works intensively with a family, and in using a range of methods to support and challenge families as necessary in order to secure change.

The TFP has given us the opportunity to make a significant difference for many families over the last two years. At a time when so many public services are being cut back it is encouraging to see Government-led investment in intensive work with families.

While Family Action supports the TFP wholeheartedly, we do not think it is perfect. There are undoubtedly families who would benefit from the intensive support that the TFP provides that have not met three out of the four criteria that have determined entry onto Phase 1 of the programme. The four criteria are as follows: involved in youth crime or anti-social behaviour (ASB) and/or with a child who is regularly truanting; and/or with an adult in the family on Department for Work and Pensions (DWP) out-of-work benefits; and/or who meet another locally determined criteria. We have lobbied hard for these entry criteria to be broadened in the second phase of the programme.

In Family Action's view the 'results' that have attracted additional 'payment' under Phase 1 of the TFP are but a subset, and quite a limited one at that, of the areas where profound change can be achieved through focused and intensive work with families. In our opinion, we need to think much more broadly when measuring success for these families. A focus on a limited subset of 'results' alone may be necessary to secure national-level investment, but it risks obscuring the journey that families take when they are helped to address longstanding difficulties. In consequence, we may diminish our understanding of how best to help them. The endless focus on counting the numbers of families identified, engaged and 'turned around' only serves to divert attention from the remarkable success that is often achieved with individual families.

Family Action was delighted when the Government announced in 2013 that the TFP would be extended into the next Parliament and that at least another £200 million would be invested to extend help to a wider group of 400,000 families following the end of Phase 1 in March 2015. It was then subsequently announced in the 2014 budget that 40,000 of these additional families would now be worked with more quickly than previously announced by Early Starter local authorities during the 2014/15 financial year. These announcements underline that the TFP will have a bigger reach in the future and that it will be working with a broader range of need. It is of course essential that the TFP continues, but it is equally important that the second phase of the programme learns the lessons from the first couple of years of delivery if it is to maximise its impact and achieve lasting change for families.

I am writing this chapter from the perspective of delivery under Phase 1 of the TFP. It has been clear since August 2014 that the entry criteria for Phase 2 of the TFP will be much broader than under Phase 1 and this is very welcome news. Entry criteria for Phase 2 will be based on a group of six headline problems and a combination of any two of these will be enough to establish eligibility. Under Phase 2 the six headline problems are:

1. Parents and children involved in crime or anti-social behaviour;

2. Children who have not been attending school regularly;

3. Children who need help;

4. Adults out of work or at risk of financial exclusion and young people at risk of worklessness;

5. Families affected by domestic violence and abuse; and

6. Parents and children with a range of health problems.

Family Action and Phase 1 of the TFP

Family Action has provided TFP services in metropolitan (e.g. in two London boroughs and in parts of Manchester, Birmingham and Sheffield) and in comparatively rural (e.g. Lincolnshire) areas across England. All of the upper tier local authorities involved in the TFP can decide their own approach to the programme and as a result we have not been commissioned to provide the same service in every area where we have worked. This is an issue in practice as it means we can work with families in some areas for longer than in others and I discuss the consequences of this variation later in this chapter.

Families receiving TFP services are often characterised as being extreme in both their levels of need and behaviour. However, in Family Action's experience the families referred to our projects differ considerably. In order to illustrate the range of work that we are carrying out under the umbrella of the TFP I set out below four case studies taken from our TFP work across the country. These case studies offer a flavour of the work that we are typically asked to do and our results. For reasons of confidentiality I have deliberately not identified the areas or specific services of these case studies and names have been changed. When you read them I would encourage you to reflect on the specifics that make each of these situations different but also to notice the themes and issues that consistently arise.

JULIE'S STORY

Mother of three, Julie, was referred to Family Action by social workers at her children's school. The school was concerned about her son's mental health. Shaun, 13, was often anxious and suffered from panic attacks. He also had very low self-esteem.

When the family had been living with Shaun's father, Julie experienced domestic abuse and subsequently received support from Social Care for problems with her mental health. This, along with Julie's alcohol misuse, had a significant impact on the children, especially Shaun, who took up the role as carer for his mother when she was going through difficult times. This is where much of Shaun's anxiety came from – he was constantly worried that his mother could be at risk of attack when he was at school.

The family's chaotic history meant all of Julie's children were unsettled. They had moved to a different town to flee their violent father and were living with Julie's mother, as they didn't have a home of their own.

Staff at Family Action worked closely with the family to identify key areas of support for Julie and her children.

The original referral information did not mention Julie's other two children; however, staff felt it was vital to factor their needs and roles into their plan in order to effectively support the family as a whole. Family Action staff also worked with selected partner agencies to ensure Julie and her children had as much help as possible.

Shaun and his older brother spent time talking to a Family Action support worker about their feelings so that they could make sense of their experiences and responsibilities at home. Shaun's older brother had a poor relationship with his father so Family Action staff worked with teachers at his school to give him space to express his negative feelings. Staff also worked with him to establish trusting relationships with specific teachers that would provide a long-term source of support and enable him to take care of his own mental health and emotional wellbeing in the future.

Family Action staff worked with Julie to help her access the right services to tackle her mental health issues. Julie started on a course of talking therapies including Cognitive Behavioural Therapy and Cognitive Analytic Therapy. The team worked intensively with her to address the amount of exposure her children had to the distress and negativity that were linked to her mental health issues. Julie was also helped to become more positive around her children and was shown ways to prevent her low self-esteem and negative outlook increasing their anxiety levels.

With support, Shaun showed significant improvements and has already become far more confident. He is happier and has a renewed sense of enjoyment about life. He told staff that he feels a lot less anxious and more settled.

Although Julie and her children are still living with Julie's mother, Family Action has worked with her to ensure she is registered with all the local housing accommodation lists. They hope to have their own home soon. Julie and Shaun's case is due to close shortly as Family Action has seen huge improvements in the family, particularly the children's emotional wellbeing. Julie is now much more confident and this can be seen clearly through the positive changes in her children.

FAITH'S STORY

Faith and her nine-year-old son Andrew were referred to Family Action due to concerns about Faith's ability to manage Andrew's disruptive and changeable behaviour. Faith was having difficulties setting and maintaining boundaries and Andrew was reluctant to accept reasonable requests. It was felt that if Andrew's behaviour continued it would have a significant negative effect on the younger extended family members and Andrew's own emotional development.

Whilst Andrew's school had not reported any problems with his attendance, the Special Educational Needs Co-ordinator did report major concerns about Andrew's behaviour and his mother's inability to set and maintain appropriate boundaries. At this point Andrew was not on a plan or programme at school to manage his behaviour, but was at risk of exclusion if his behaviour did not significantly improve. Andrew had no known health issues and he was accessing help from the Child and Adolescent Mental Health Service (CAMHS), which included therapeutic support and a psychiatric assessment.

Faith was very resistant to any interventions at first as she felt that Andrew was just extremely naughty because he was missing his father. She believed that this was why it proved difficult for the sanctions to work for Andrew and why she failed to maintain the boundaries she set.

When Family Action allocated Faith a Family Support Worker they discussed various ways in which they could support her and Andrew to get things back on track. Faith said she would embrace any suggestions of support as she was seriously worried that Andrew would be excluded from school and also be isolated from the extended family because of his behaviour.

The Family Support Worker agreed twice weekly sessions for Faith at Andrew's school. They attended these meetings with Faith so that she felt confident and supported in agreeing interventions and improvements for dealing with Andrew's behaviour. The Family Support Worker organised monthly feedback for Faith regarding Andrew's progress.

Faith was also helped to devise simple routines to assist her in keeping Andrew's behaviour under control. They introduced a play, praise, sanctions and rewards chart that was monitored by the Family Support Worker on a weekly basis.

The Family Support Worker identified that Faith had been having difficulty securing a job. She believed that as well as working on changing Andrew's behaviour it would help Faith and Andrew's relationship if Faith could find work. The Family Support Worker referred Faith to Jobcentre Plus and supported her in looking for work.

Since working with Faith, Andrew's school has reported that it now has fewer concerns about Andrew's behaviour. Although they will continue monitoring him for a short while, it was noted that Andrew is meeting his attainment levels and has a warm and loving relationship with his mother and extended family members. Andrew has begun to attend his local mosque on Fridays with family friends and is learning Arabic. He is also in contact with his estranged father. He sees him every two weeks and really enjoys spending special time with him.

Faith has now secured a job at a primary school as an After School Assistant and is very happy with her achievements.

PAULA'S STORY

Paula's family was well known to local support services, but she had always refused to engage with them. The local school also had difficulty engaging with Paula and had concerns about the welfare and emotional wellbeing of her children. The school was unclear about the children's relationship with their father and how much contact they were supposed to have with him. Concerns were raised about the children's safety after Paula ceased supervised contact with the children and their father, and did not provide any details about future contact to the school.

When Family Action started to work with Paula she was heavily pregnant and living at the top of a block of flats, which did not have a working lift. The family home had no heating or hot water, and a broken cooker meant that Paula was unable to prepare hot meals for the family. The house was bare and lacked any kind of stimulation or feeling of homeliness. Most of the doors had broken hinges, so the flat was also unsafe.

Family Action supported Paula and her children in a variety of ways. First of all, the Family Support Worker arranged one-to-one sessions with each child at their school, providing them with a safe space to discuss their feelings and strengthen relationships with their teachers. The Family Support Worker was able to negotiate a subsidy for after-school provision for the youngest children, and Paula also received support in finding more positive ways to communicate with her children about their feelings when they were at home.

The Family Support Worker completed grant applications for a cooker, beds and a buggy for the new baby. They also liaised with housing, heating and utility providers to rectify the issues with the heating and hot water. They attended court and provided supporting statements which meant that Paula and her children were not evicted from their home. Paula was also encouraged to attend Team Around the Child meetings at her children's school, which significantly improved her relationship with the staff there.

Family Action provided toys and activities for the children to help improve their emotional and social development. This in turn had an effect on Paula and really helped with her emotional wellbeing.

Since Family Action started working with Paula, the children have started to improve their performance at school and are forming better relationships with their classmates. Their attendance and punctuality have improved significantly and they are also getting involved in positive activities outside of school. They have re-established regular contact with their father, which is being managed with help from Family Action. Paula has also been able to access education and training and is really enjoying learning new skills.

When the Family Support Worker asked Paula and her children for feedback on the support they had received one of her children said: 'I felt happy because I got to share all of my feelings, I am now an excellent communicator!'

JANE'S STORY

Jane was referred to Family Action because of her son Michael's poor attendance at school and his challenging behaviour. Jane was struggling with setting and managing boundaries, as Michael would not listen or follow rules. Michael had been excluded from school and Jane was suffering from depression and anxiety. Whilst Michael was receiving support from CAMHS, their relationship had broken down many times. Jane told Family Action that she couldn't put into words how upsetting and stressful the situation was; she just didn't know what to do any more.

Jane was allocated a Family Support Worker who helped her learn techniques to manage Michael's behaviour and be more consistent with boundaries. The Family Support Worker had one-to-one sessions with Michael so that he could talk about his feelings and also supported him to attend his CAMHS appointments. Michael had support to improve his attendance at school and the Family Support Worker helped him with his transition back into school full time. Jane also had advice and help on how to access information and support groups for Oppositional Defiant Disorder to help her understand and cope more effectively with Michael's behaviour.

Over the six months that Family Action worked with Jane there was a huge improvement in Michael's behaviour and attitude. He took on board advice and criticism during discussions with the Family Support Worker and worked on being more positive. Michael found a school that he would like to attend and began a placement in order to make the move. Michael attended all his CAMHS appointments and was reported to be doing really well. He also made the decision to stop hanging around with people who were a negative influence on him, and since that point his behaviour really changed for the better. The Family Support Worker also helped Michael find activities he could take part in outside of school. He started a weekend free-running class, which he really enjoys.

Jane said: 'Things have got so much better. Michael is going to school every day and is so much happier. It's like he looks forward to getting up in the morning, I don't even need to wake him up. I feel more confident dealing with his behaviour now, and I know that I need to make sure I stay consistent. I hadn't ever thought about the future before because I always had issues with Michael and had to take each day as it came. I've had support to build a CV and hopefully in the future I can start volunteering and looking at part-time work. I am also starting an anxiety relaxation course to help deal with my own anxiety.'

Discussion

When I read these case studies I am struck by the repeated mentions of anxiety, low self-esteem and concern for the emotional wellbeing of adults and children. Concern about parenting effectiveness is also a persistent theme. Issues about children's poor behaviour and attendance at school, significant housing issues, long-term unemployment, difficult couple relationships and relationships between parents and their children and between absent fathers and their children all come up more than once. Other serious contextual factors such as domestic abuse, substance misuse and poverty feature in individual cases.

These case studies illustrate the range of need that we encounter when working with the families and the reality that changing just one thing for the better is unlikely to change the trajectory for a family or to 'turn them around'.

It is Family Action's aim to make a profound and lasting difference. Experience tells us that it is a practical, hands-on, whole family approach that is most effective at tackling enduring issues such as anxiety, parenting challenges and low self-esteem.

Evidence of impact against the TFP Payment by Results outcome measures

Across all of Family Action's TFP provision we have tended to see good results in decreasing ASB and youth offending and in increasing school attendance. Across our TFP services we have worked hard to support families to make progress towards work but we have often struggled to help our families find continuous employment within the timescale of the commissioned service. We think this is unsurprising given the issues that often need to be resolved before work can become a realistic goal. It is important that we avoid helping people to get into unsuitable jobs just to achieve the payment for this outcome. That will not help in the long term and does not make financial sense; in fact the family can go backwards as the bad experience will put them off applying for a job in future. We want to see people in appropriate jobs that they will want to keep. If that means taking longer to prepare them for work then that is the right thing to do.

Our experience across our TFP services, coupled with our considerable experience of successful family intervention, suggests that families often need other issues (housing, repairs, mental health [particularly anxiety and depression], domestic abuse, other relationship issues, debt, substance misuse etc.) to be addressed before they can even think about, let alone achieve, the national Payment by Results outcomes.

Broader impact of Family Action's TFP services

Families have engaged well with all of our services and we have been careful to adapt individual services to tackle local issues. We have also seen evidence of more joined-up working with other agencies as a result of the TFP. Although it is not a national TFP outcome area, Family Action has seen a significant level of improvement in parenting capacity in families and we can evidence that improvement. In every Family Action TFP service we have used the Family Star Plus (an outcomes tool that measures parenting effectiveness) in order to engage families with our services, identify priority areas to be addressed and measure their journey and progress over the course of our time with them. Figure 2.1 illustrates how the Family Star Plus captures the progress made by a family from initial assessment to closure of the case across a range of dimensions of parenting.

In Family Action's experience, families in our TFP services can also make great strides forward in other areas, for example via improvements in family relationships, connection to the community, accessing services that will help them back into work, self-belief, aspiration, resilience, reduction in ongoing need for social care, reduction in interpersonal/domestic violence etc. We think it is a shame that such progress does not attract a Payment by Results payment under Phase 1 of the TFP, but we are more concerned by the fact that these individual successes are not systematically captured at national level. This risks skewing our understanding of the impact of the TFP as a whole.

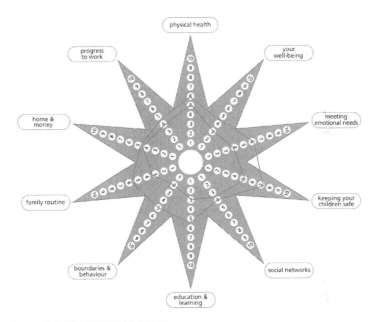

FIGURE 2.1 FAMILY STAR PLUS

Challenges in providing Phase 1 of the TFP on the ground

The criteria for the inclusion of families and measurement of success of the programme needed to be broader

Many local authorities have recognised that domestic abuse, mental health and parenting capacity are important factors in making a difference to these families and have included these issues within local criteria. However, provider organisations cannot be paid for achieving outcomes in these areas. We know that for the families we work with these are big issues – over half of families in one of our services are affected by domestic abuse and 75 per cent in another have mental health issues. For success in national outcomes these issues must also be recognised and tackled.

We have found it difficult in some areas to find sufficient families with the three criteria necessary to access the service under Phase 1; often families have two. These families could actually be supported through early intervention work to avoid them reaching three criteria. For example, one referral we received had two parents working, yet their son was in a gang and in a lot of trouble. The family had many stresses to cope with, but were not a high priority for the TFP. However, if the young man was also involved in ASB or crime due to his gang involvement then the family would meet the TFP criteria. We worked with this family anyway, as the young man's behaviour also influenced two other boys from troubled families. In future, the impact that families have on others, despite not meeting education, work, crime or local criteria, should arguably be included in the programme criteria.

In contrast, some of the referrals received meet the TFP criteria but do not need the level of intensive family support that the programme is designed to deliver. It could be argued that this is a form of early intervention, but it may make more financial sense to provide those families with a lower level service and save funds for those that need high-level support. For example, a referral was received in one of our services from a senior school about the attendance of a young man, which was at 78 per cent. The family consisted of Mum, her 14-year-old son and her two-year-old daughter. Mum was not working, as she had her daughter to care for and was planning to retrain when she needed to return to work. The young man played football for a large, professional team's youth team and therefore had productive use of his leisure time, as well as meeting a mentor once per week. His home conditions were very good and his mum needed to do some work on implementing boundaries, but this was not a major problem. When trying to agree a plan, we struggled to justify the need for twice-weekly visits, particularly given the mentor's involvement with the young man. In addition, Payment by Results meant that we needed to work with the family for a minimum of two months. In this case, failure to meet the target of achieving 85 per cent school attendance was not necessarily evidence that the family was troubled.

Contractual end dates can also be an issue with Payment by Results, for example one local authority highlighted to us that there was an issue with the education additional payment for a TFP service that we were contracted to provide until March 2015. It said that any referral received by us after April 2014 based on educational attendance would not be eligible for the additional payment, even if we are successful in gaining 100 per cent attendance, as there would not be three full terms of data available to prove the outcome! We challenged this on the basis that that the TFP programme is being extended into 2015/16.

The programme should cater for different levels of need, with step-up and step-down services

All of our TFP services last for different lengths of time: in one area they last three to six months, in a second area six months and in a third area over a year. However, given the difficulties these families face, three to six months is not long to build trust with the family or for someone who has been out of work for 15 years to get a job, and those who do find a job will not necessarily stay in it after the intervention. In Family Action's experience, families achieve better outcomes when there is follow-up support and we would like to see a greater emphasis on ensuring that step-down services are available in order to sustain the progress made by families. In our experience, not many families are at the violent extreme that often characterises the TFP – we need a flexible service to reflect the different levels of need. Some families require very intensive family support with one key worker delivering all the support whilst others benefit from different models of intervention such as group work provision or peer support. It is important that we can flex the TFP in order to meet the assessed needs of individual families and to make the available funding stretch as far as it possibly can.

The way the programme is commissioned by some local authorities is problematic

In more than one local authority area, the TFP Phase 1 tendering exercise use of Payment by Results conditions meant we would only receive 60 per cent of the estimated cost of the service in the second year of service provision if we did not reach the national outcomes. This was irrespective of what else was achieved through the service in terms of other outcomes for individual families. This would not be enough to cover salary costs, and for a charity without substantial reserves it presents an unaffordable risk meaning that we are unlikely even to bid for the work even though we are very well placed to do it.

It is worrying if the market to provide these services is being skewed by imposing unnecessary financial risk.

In contrast, some local authorities choose to contract with voluntary sector organisations to deliver the national outcomes, but on a non Payment by Results basis, thereby taking the risk themselves. The answer probably lies somewhere in the middle; it is reasonable to expect voluntary sector organisations to take some financial risk, but not all of it.

Some of the issues targeted by the programme, such as worklessness, are influenced by other agencies, meaning that Payment by Results can be unduly affected. One local authority informed us that if the council could not find the full amount of families to refer to us, we would be expected to deliver support to other families, without the additional Payment by Results money! Given the variation in practice that we have seen, there must be scope here for the Department for Communities and Local Government (DCLG) to consider issuing guidance on the effective commissioning of the TFP. This could usefully address issues such as the outsourcing of financial risk.

Organisations should be paid on a step-change basis not ultimate goals

Our Family Star Plus outcomes tool can measure the progress made over the course of a time-limited intervention with a family.

In our experience, the journey towards improved outcomes is just as important as the end results achieved. For example, the average Family Star Plus for one of our services showed that over the six months in terms of parenting effectiveness, families tended to move from 'stuck' to 'trying to change' – they had not yet completely succeeded. In another service, the local authority allows a parent going into education to be enough to get the payment for a successful work outcome.

The name of the programme should be changed

The name 'Troubled Families' is dispiriting to families, and does not encourage them to engage. The name gives the TFP a punitive image and does not accurately reflect the situation of many of the families. Someone suffering domestic abuse, but also identified as a member of a troubled family, is less likely to engage with an agency that is putting such a label on the family. These families often have complex needs, but they are not necessarily 'trouble'. Many local authorities have avoided using the term 'troubled' because of the stigma attached. As a result, we work in services called Think Families, Families Working Together, Families First, etc.

We need to be able to work with other agencies more effectively

Data-sharing issues with other agencies have hindered the ability of Family Action key workers to make and measure progress. Many agencies are worried about data protection rules. These are not new issues and extensive guidance has been given in the past to overcome these difficulties, but it continues to be a problem on the ground. Again, there could be a role here for DCLG to issue clear guidance not just on the vexed issue of data sharing but particularly on the issue of sharing risk assessment information, as without this, staff and service users are potentially put in danger. We also continue to encounter issues in terms of how much schools, GP practices and other relevant services are aware of the programme. We have witnessed some excellent practice in terms of promoting the TFP locally and would like to see this everywhere. Sharing Payment by Results payments between partners in recognition of successful joint or sequential work, for example in helping someone get into employment, may provide a way forward but could also be bureaucratic in practice. TFP partnerships across the country are thinking this through and we need to keep sharing our delivery experience. In Family Action's experience, the more we can do to build shared responsibility for outcomes between agencies, the better. In a similar vein, there is undoubtedly scope to train key workers further, for example to help them to recognise certain health issues or to respond consistently to family conflict/domestic abuse and this could make them even more effective in role. The point here is that a programme like TFP is always going to be dynamic – with so many services across England and so much developing experience there will be always be good practice to share and new ways to make the TFP even better.

Shaping Phase 2 of the TFP – what would Family Action like to see in the future?

The experience of delivering a range of TFP services across the country has led me to reflect deeply with colleagues delivering these programmes on the ground on the payments by results criteria used under Phase 1 of the TFP and how these might be modified now that we know the programme is to be expanded.

We have witnessed significant success for school attendance, reduction of exclusions and general family functioning in the TFP services we deliver across England. However, as I submitted at the Public Accounts Committee hearing when I gave evidence on the TFP, there are challenges presented by the current Payment by Results criteria in terms of what is measured and over what period of time.

We believe that it is important that the Payment by Results criteria incorporate progress measures as well as end goals, especially when services are commissioned for short periods of time or families have taken a long time to engage with the service. In our experience, the journey towards improved outcomes is just as important as the end result and can save money for taxpayers in the long term.

Related to these progress indicators is the importance of finding ways to include measurement and payment for families that continue to progress or achieve the final stage of the Payment by Results criteria after the intervention period. We think this would encourage value for money and sustainability of the programme by ensuring that delivery organisations help families achieve the best progress they can. Such incremental improvements will be more deeply rooted and sustainable and these should be the goal, rather than being driven by actions that will receive the payments needed to continue running the service. For example, it may work better for more people to achieve progression into work during the intervention, with full employment and a related payment achieved a year later, rather than, for example, rushing a parent into an inappropriate job that they may leave after the service has stopped supporting them and which discourages them from entering other fields of work.

In some cases our services are contracted to work with families for only six months. It is very difficult to achieve the current employment criteria in this time, given that the current cohort of parents are likely to have been unemployed for a significant period and a large amount of the intervention period can be spent getting families to engage. Indeed, if it is achieved, and for the intervention to be sustained, the parent is likely to need further ongoing support. We think it would be better to require evidence that individuals have had support to become more job-ready.

We believe it should be acknowledged that it is not just involvement in the Work Programme that shows progress towards work. Progress towards work should be valued more and attract greater recognition, whether achieved through individuals attending employability courses, interview preparation sessions, becoming involved in volunteering or enrolling in further education etc. These indicators can be measured using data from the job centre where necessary.

We believe the education criterion should be reduced to a time period of less than three terms for both eligibility and outcome. The current criterion does not adequately allow emerging issues to be picked up and means that by the time the eligibility criteria is met, absence issues can be significantly entrenched. In addition, for some of our services, the three school terms criteria for the outcomes measure excludes young people entering the service in their final year. Given that the extended programme is looking to intervene in families where issues have not reached the severity of the initial cohort of families, we believe this change is necessary for the programme's continued success and sustainability. Where children reach school leaving age, we suggest that a payment is made if they then go on to progress along the pathway to work, using the measures suggested above.

There are additional areas that are often covered by local authorities in their local inclusion criteria but do not qualify for Payment by Results. According to the National Audit Office, 'over 50 per cent of local authorities used domestic violence or abuse, drugs, alcohol or substance misuse, and mental health for their local criteria' (Department for Communities and Local Government and the Department for Work and Pensions 2013). We know that for the families with whom we work, these are big issues. We think these areas need to be included in the criteria in future, as it is difficult to succeed with the current outcomes criteria without providing support and making progress on these issues.

For the issue of domestic abuse, we would suggest an outcome measure of 'Has there been a domestic abuse incident in the last six weeks (to which the police were called)?' This measure is currently used in one of our services as part of the locally defined criteria. An alternative would be to release payment if a 60 per cent reduction in domestic abuse incidents, as reported by the police, is achieved. We recognise that many domestic abuse incidents go unreported, so would also suggest that a progress measure is used as part of the Payment by Results criteria. For example, we use the Empowerment Star, which notes improvements in safety, support networks, empowerment and self-esteem, among other aspects, on a scale of one to ten.

In the area of mental health, it is suggested that an improved wellbeing score, or reduced anxiety and depression score from a recognised clinical tool, would be a valuable outcomes measure for individuals on the programme. Our services that measure mental health related outcomes currently use the Hospital Anxiety and

Depression Scale to assess progress. As a clinical tool widely used by GPs, this offers a robust method of measuring results. It is suggested that this questionnaire should be completed fortnightly to measure progress, and that Payment by Results should be released as progress stages are met.

As substance or alcohol misuse may be related to these mental health issues, and impact upon the family, it would also be good to have a similar outcomes measure that reflects this. For example, 'percentage reduction in substance/alcohol misuse from initial baseline per month' could be used as an outcomes measure, with organisations achieving progress payments, but only receiving each stage's payment once per individual.

The current TFP does not measure parenting capacity, although an improvement in this is, in the vast majority of cases, needed to impact on the Payment by Results outcomes. In many of our family support services we have used the Family Star Plus outcomes tool to measure progress on parenting capacity, as well as progress towards other relevant areas for the TFP. The areas assessed on a scale of one to ten are boundary setting, routine setting, keeping children safe, providing home and money, supporting learning, promoting good health and engaging in supportive social networks. Separate scales also look at supporting children's emotional wellbeing, parents' emotional wellbeing and parents' progress to work. As this tool is based on scales, an outcomes measure could base payment on incremental progress along these over the length of the intervention.

Additionally, the current inclusion criteria do not identify families with problems who have children below school age and or below the age of criminal responsibility. Suggested Payment by Results outcomes measures that could include these families are: improved engagement with health visiting services, improved attendance at nursery provision or reduction in excessive parental use of primary or secondary health care.

It would also be helpful to have Payment by Results criteria that focus more explicitly on adult offending, as this is often an indicator of future direction for young people in the family. A suggested outcomes measure would be a 33 per cent reduction in offending over the last six months, in line with the current Payment by Results criterion for offending by minors.

With all of these suggestions there would be considerable scope for DCLG to identify acceptable alternative measurement tools. We understand the need to make the measurement of progress as robust as possible.

It is important to note that the Government announced in August 2014 that under Phase 2 of the TFP results based payments will be simplified and offered for each family for whom the local authority claims to have either (a) achieved significant and sustained progress, or (b) moved off out of work benefits and into continuous employment. In principle this broadening out of the Payment By Results criteria is again welcome and we expect this to translate through into how providers are in turn paid by results under Phase 2. The reality of course is that none of us will really be able to judge how the new approach to Payment By Results is working in practice until well into 2015 but the direction of travel looks promising in permitting a broader interpretation of how progress is evidenced. The Government has also indicated that it wants to capture a much richer understanding of the progress achieved with a representative sample of families through the TFP via Family Monitoring Data. As I have argued throughout this chapter it is crucial to develop a deeper understanding of the progress that families can make on a number of fronts as a result of an effective TFP intervention – we must understand that progress in the round if we are to judge the impact of the TFP properly. I also note that the Government has said that it wants to develop a much better understanding of the financial benefits achieved through the Phase 2 of the TPF and how this contributes to service transformation. Again this is vital if we are fully to understand the impact of the programme.

Conclusion

The TFP is already making a significant difference to many families, but to achieve its potential as a platform for system change as well as family level change, the second phase of the programme needs to continue to learn from the early delivery experience. I have described some of the challenges of working with the TFP in Phase 1 in this chapter and also a range of potential solutions. These solutions were shared in good time with the Troubled Families Unit at the DCLG and I have been encouraged by the Government's announcements about the broadening of the entry criteria and the payments by results measures that will be used in Phase 2 that have been made in recent months. With a larger number of families to be supported and less funding per family in Phase 2 we will all need time to work under the new system before we can judge how it is working in practice but the broadening out of the criteria certainly feels right to me.

The Government has a long-term vision of changing the balance on spend on troubled families from crisis response and management to early intervention and prevention. Family Action wholeheartedly shares that vision but we also recognise that it will require long-term cross-party support at both national and local levels, continuing targeted investment in prevention and early intervention and the actual redistribution of savings from current spend further down the line if it is to be achieved. Achieving the Government's vision also requires a very strong focus on building resilience at all levels: personal resilience, for example good adaptive coping skills; economic resilience, for example the ability to secure and hold down a job; resilient families, for example the ability to weather the vicissitudes of life and resilient communities that work together for the common good.

We will need to keep flexing the TFP over time as we learn from the experience of delivering it on the ground, and our approach needs to be holistic, intergenerational and long term. For me, the number of families identified who are provided with a service and who achieve the specified national outcomes in Phase 1 are not the key measures of success however important they might have been in securing cross-Government investment. I am more interested in whether we identified the right families and offered them the right interventions at the right times in their lives. I am just as interested in the totality of change that we have achieved for those families as a result of the TFP.

I have argued in this chapter that we need to be more flexible in how we view and measure success – the national outcomes are, of course, important but so are the incremental steps that families take on their individual journeys under the TFP. Achieving change in specific, measured areas is impressive but we need to ensure that we understand the full range of change that has been achieved so that we can ensure that that success is captured and that it can be sustained. In Family Action's experience, the needs of the whole family need to be assessed and kept in mind if change is to become embedded.

Early intervention and prevention must be prioritised in universal settings if we are really to change the balance of spend over time but, in Family Action's view, there will always be a role for intensive work in the family home for those families who need one-on-one support, a role model to follow and someone to provide the impetus for lasting change.

Family Action's experience over many years is that some families will always need this support and will not be able to change without it. That is why we support the TFP and what it is seeking to achieve for families across England and why we will do all that we can to help the programme to succeed as it moves into Phase 2.

Reference

Department for Communities and Local Government and the Department for Work and Pensions (2013) *Programmes to Help Families Facing Multiple Challenges.* London: The Stationery Office.

Department for Communities and Local Government. (2014) *Financial Framework for the Expanded Troubled Families Programme.* London: DCLG.

HM Treasury, The Rt Hon Danny Alexander MP, The Rt Hon Eric Pickles MP and Department for Communities and Local Government (2013) *Massive Expansion of Troubled Families Programme Announced.* www.gov.uk/government/news/massive-expansion-of-troubled-families-programme-announced, accessed on 2 Feburary 2015.

CHAPTER 3

The Troubled Families Workforce and Occupational Identity

DR SADIE PARR, SHEFFIELD HALLAM UNIVERSITY

Introduction

Over the last decade it is what is broadly referred to as 'intensive family intervention' that has emerged as the key technology in the governance of families defined as having multiple and complex needs. This approach was first consolidated in the New Labour Government's (1997–2010) 2006 *Respect Action Plan*, which committed the then Government to establishing a network of Family Intervention Projects (FIPs) (Respect Task Force 2006). Since coming to power in the 2010 UK general election, the Liberal–Conservative Coalition Government has remained committed to the continuation and expansion of this method of working as part of the 'troubled family' programme in which the 152 upper tier local authorities in England are expected to 'turn around' the lives of an estimated 120,000 families defined as having multiple problems by new or existing programmes over three years (April 2012 to May 2015). These families are characterised by there being no adult in the family working, children not being in school and family members being involved in crime and anti-social behaviour (ASB). The criteria also include a degree of local discretion so that councils can target the families that they feel would benefit from intensive intervention.

Successive Governments' commitment to this model of working has been driven by evidence derived from evaluations that have consistently provided findings to demonstrate that intensive interventions are effective in bringing about change for the most vulnerable families (DCLG 2012; Natcen 2010; Nixon *et al.* 2006; White *et al.* 2008). Specialist, intensive and long-term support tailored to children's and families' particular needs is consequently now considered to be best practice and is central to the delivery of children's and family services. At the heart of this model of working is a dedicated Family Intervention Worker (FIW) who manages a small case load and is able to provide an intensive level of contact with a family over a prolonged period. This worker is expected to assess the family's needs, develop support plans and coordinate the delivery of services. They both deliver support to families directly and refer them on to specialist interventions. They are often institutionally located within specific services such as FIPs (run by the statutory or independent sector), although in some locations the approach has been mainstreamed as the main mechanism for delivering services to the most vulnerable children and families (Batty *et al.* 2013).

The predominance of intensive family intervention has given rise to a new and expanding occupational role within the children and families workforce, that of the 'family intervention key worker' (also referred to locally as key worker, project worker, support worker). As the Government recognises, this: 'is tough, difficult work that not everyone will be cut out to do – and doing it well, whilst staying motivated, requires training and supervision' (DCLG 2012, p.30). The family intervention key worker is not a professional role, however (it has a non-registered status and lacks professional regulation). Moreover, the overriding message has been that the possession of a particular professional qualification, vocational training or occupational background is not vital and that equally, or even more, important are personal qualities (Hayden and Jenkins 2013; Nixon *et al.* 2006; White *et al.* 2008). Evaluation reports and good practice guides have listed the attitudes, personal qualities and styles of working that have been identified as important for effective and productive work with families. These include having good interpersonal and communication skills, being non-judgemental, honest, determined and consistent, resilient, tenacious, positive, patient, and having energy and enthusiasm (DCLG 2012; Nixon *et al.* 2006; White *et al.* 2008). As such, key workers are drawn from a range of occupational backgrounds, including housing management, social care, education and youth justice, with very different qualifications and levels of experience. Some key workers may be recruited on the basis of strong interpersonal skills and the ability to engage with potentially hard to reach families and have no qualifications, while other key workers may be qualified social workers or have a vocational degree in Youth and Community Work (Children's Workforce Development Council (CWDC) 2012). Furthermore, some intensive family intervention services are professionally homogeneous and might, for instance, be run by teams of FIWs all with similar occupational backgrounds, while others are multidisciplinary, something often viewed as advantageous on the grounds that skills sets usefully complement each other (CWDC 2012).

Over the last couple of years, the Government has begun to address the issue of key worker training and there is now an NVQ Level 4 in Work with Parents (Working with Families with Multiple and Complex Needs), which was developed to support the training and development of FIWs. Not all local authorities use this, however, and some have developed locally specific in-house training and supervision programmes to support the key worker role. What this reflects and what is striking about the makeup of the workforce is that there is no consistency across the country in terms of the occupational identity of key workers nor is there standardisation of practice or role remit. It is a workforce that is defined by diversity.

There is a body of work that has quite rightly unpicked the attitudes, personal qualities and styles of working that have been identified by project staff and families as important in family intervention work. The impact of professional or occupational identities, skills and competencies however has been sorely neglected.

This omission is remiss: intensive family support is relationship-based work, meaning that good interpersonal skills are imperative, but so too are professional competencies. Questions remain therefore about training, quality, management and supervision, as well as professional ideology and boundaries. FIWs are required to collate and process complex (sometimes competing) information about people and their lives and take appropriate courses of action to help them bring about change. Assessing and responding appropriately to children and families with multiple and complex needs requires specialist skills and knowledge and differentially qualified FIWs are likely to undertake such work in diverse ways. There needs to be an assurance that the families are being supported by FIWs appropriately trained to deal with the complexities they may face. Likewise, it is important that managers ensure that the demands placed on 'unqualified' and inexperienced staff are not outwith their remit nor unduly high.

The chapter begins with a brief introduction to family intervention projects and the key worker approach theorised as being central to the success of the projects. The following two sections then discuss two FIPs. Both were set up as ASB FIPs in the early 2000s. Evaluative studies of these projects included qualitative interviews with families, staff and key partners. The research studies both touched on the issue of key worker skills, competencies and qualifications and emerged as an important topic that demands deeper exploration. The research is indicative of the ways in which professional identifies and practices affect how intensive interventions works. This chapter is not intended to be a discussion of concrete 'findings' that can be read as empirical claims but is primarily illustrative and exploratory. My hope is that it opens up this neglected area of study to further debate and to empirical and theoretical development. Particular attention is paid to how the key worker is positioned in relation to social work and the extent to which support should be regarded as a form of social work.

Family projects

Families referred to intensive family intervention projects are characterised as having multiple and complex support needs. FIPs seek to help families determine what needs to change in order for them to improve their situation and make positive changes. This involves project workers trying to understand a set of complex, multiple and, often, entrenched needs, in order to develop individual 'support plans' for each family and, sometimes, each family member. Although projects differ and are dependent on a range of contextual factors, it is possible to point to some features that are common to most. The approach to intensive family intervention has been described in guidance as having the following critical features (CWDC 2011, p.15):

- recruitment and retention of high-quality staff with a range of experiences and backgrounds

- a key worker model to ensure families' engagement and trust and enable the family to feel responsible to the worker

- small case loads of five or six families at one time

- a whole family approach

- stay involved as long as necessary

- the use of sanctions with support

- the scope to use resources creatively

- effective multi-agency relationships.

The packages of support provided usually involve a mix of methods according to the family's and family members' unique needs. The Government endorses an approach that combines both 'support' and 'challenge': 'Family intervention workers make it clear that they have to either take this intensive help or face tough consequence' (DCLG 2012). It may comprise a combination of:

- practical assistance in the home

- provision of advice and advocacy support

- signposting to other relevant services

- providing out-of-school activities

- help in managing finances and claiming benefits

- personal skills development and 'parenting skills' training.

It is commonly felt that there is an emphasis on the projects' micro-level management of families' lifestyles as a key part of the solution in which workers might help parent/s (families are commonly headed by single parent women) establish morning and bedtime routines, make sure the house is kept in an adequate condition and encourage families to eat a healthy diet. What may be described broadly as 'informal techniques' or processes (Prior 2007) are also a key part of the intervention and exist alongside the more specific technologies discussed above. These techniques coalesce around the provision of emotional support, conversation, guidance, counselling and 'befriending'. Although these project traits are fairly common across the board, how these technologies of support are implemented and the weight given to each varies by project depending, in part, on the professional ethos of the project and the professional 'habitus' of the staff – 'the cultural, emotional and instrumental repertoires and dispositions for cognition and action' (Stenson 2005, p.274) – as well as where the project is placed within the local institutional landscape. If we are to understand contemporary FIPs and the factors that facilitate or encumber intensive family casework, we need to begin to explore the impact of the competing claims of 'professional' expertise. At this point in the chapter I want to reflect on two case studies and the issues I believe they highlight.

THE WESTCITY PROJECT: A 'SOCIAL WORK' ETHOS

The Westcity Project is a local authority FIP. The key workers all have considerable experience working as social care professionals having been previously employed in local authority social work, education welfare or youth work. It was initially designed and established by local authority social work staff and is managed by a senior social worker with experience of running family support projects. A 'social work ethos' was said to dominate within the service. Key workers, while not necessarily being qualified social workers, were encouraged to adopt a value base and associated professional practices that are compatible with those that underpin social work. Strong practice principles underpinned and created a framework for the delivery of intensive support; there were clear ideas about what constitutes 'good' practice. This gave rise to a model of working whereby family interventions were delivered within a positive context and support staff described actively avoiding top-down methods of intervention during one-to-one work, which might entail a corrective or punitive approach. Rather, project workers tried to focus on the strengths within a family, on competencies rather than 'problems' – a 'solution orientated' rather than 'problem orientated' approach.

It was clear from interviews with families that staff were able to gain the confidence of the families they supported and engage with them on an emotional level. Families felt that they were being actively listened to in a non-judgemental manner and this was significant in the development of a productive relationship. It was recognised that the approach of the support workers was assertive and project staff explained a need to be 'challenging', 'bolshy' and 'forceful' at times, and families admitted that the support workers 'pushed' them, but this was seen as non-confrontational encouragement. It was managed in a caring manner. Indeed, families did not describe any part of working with the project in negative terms and support workers suggested that they very rarely needed to employ 'the stick', which was the threat of legal action or 'sanction'. Project workers explained that 'befriending' families and being 'supportive', 'non-confrontational' and 'calm' 'worked' with families and was important in effecting engagement and positive outcomes. Despite the emphasis on dialogue and the quality of the relationship, support workers were careful to ensure relationships with families remained professional. Particular strategies were employed in order to keep clear boundaries when a relationship was at risk of getting 'too personal', which avoided dependency becoming an issue. This was confirmed by the families who took part in the research, all of whom valued highly the relationship with their support worker but were also clear that the relationship was a professional one and not a friendship.

Key workers' decisions about courses of actions were based on their interactions with families and were a response to assessments regarding family needs. When making judgements, support workers were said to operate with a high level of discretion. In so doing, project staff were able to perform their role in a way that was said to be reminiscent of 'traditional social work'. Local authority social workers were described as having little opportunity to solve problems creatively, given the constraints placed on them by a managerial and bureaucratic system that was identified as 'highly procedural and risk adverse' and 'very legalistic'. Rather than providing holistic assessments and solutions, interviewees felt that social services tended to address their intervention through the lens of child protection concerns, which could leave some issues, such as hands-on family support, unaddressed. By contrast, the space afforded to key workers to be creative and flexible was identified as its 'greatest power' and the project manager actively tried to cultivate a practice approach that encouraged creativity and innovation. However, the project manager and partner agencies were adamant that whether or not this power was effective was dependent on the skills, knowledge and professionalism of support workers who were essentially occupying ground previously inhabited by social workers. According to participants, the ability of FIP staff to be 'creative' relied on levels of confidence and self-belief in interpreting, analysing and making decisions, which is founded, at least in part, on professional training as well as effective supervision. This meant that support workers required particular types of knowledge and skills in order to make sense of and respond appropriately to emotionally sensitive and complex situations. As such, while it was recognised that communication skills and personal attributes were vital qualities required in key workers, Westcity Project's management staff explained their commitment to employing key workers with relatively high levels of qualifications and experience with the rationale that offering low salaries would not attract the high-calibre candidates that the positions required; i.e. 'You get what you pay for.'

In order to attract and retain such highly skilled staff, a strategic decision had been taken to offer salaries higher than those offered to FIP staff elsewhere in the UK and comparable to those paid to experienced social workers. This was in recognition that the support worker role is challenging, complex and demanding, and as such the management team 'wanted the best'. Support workers were generally not newly qualified, had relevant experience and were highly skilled and had to be educated to at least degree level. This was considered as entirely appropriate given the complex and high-level welfare support needs that characterised the large majority of the families referred. The Project Manager (himself an experienced and senior social worker) also described a 'liaising culture' where key workers were supported by senior staff and regular review sessions that allowed space for reflection on cases and the emotional challenges key workers may be facing. This provision of supervision was seen as crucial for maintaining standards and protecting the wellbeing of key workers. This point was confirmed by project staff, who pointed to an organisational context in which collegial relationships, ample training and reflective relationships prevailed.

The skill levels of the staff had an impact on the type of interventions provided to families. It meant that support workers themselves were able to provide specialist intervention directly, such as family therapy and counselling, and regularly supported families to address specific needs such as alcohol or substance misuse, domestic violence and anger management. While the project workers commonly tackled complex deep-seated issues, they were less likely to provide support around financial management, practical assistance in the home and accessing training/work. Project workers also tried to ensure that their role was clear and that duplication of effort was avoided; this sometimes meant that social services withdrew support or reduced their contact time with the family but this seemed to be achieved in a mutually agreeable way. In fact, the project was described as being effective in taking the lead role in coordinating agency involvement with the family. This latter role was perhaps made possible because of both the level of expertise of the staff and the project's high profile. The Westcity Project was said to be well embedded in the institutional landscape of community safety and children's services and, without exception, partner agencies described good working relationships with the service at both a strategic and service-delivery level. This is not to say that partnership working was and had always been seamless or tension free. The Project Manager acknowledged that, 'pure social work values don't sit easily with the project', explaining that the service had been established to address somewhat competing priorities given the community-focused nature of the ASB agenda. The Project Manager was engaged in strategic work to ensure the project had a valued place within the local policy and practice context and that its remit spoke to the priorities of other agencies. It was felt, however, that the project manager had been successful in publicising and clearly articulating the work of the project in part through his active membership of a number of multi-agency panels and partnerships forums.

THE NORTHCITY PROJECT:
A HOUSING APPROACH

Whereas a 'social work' culture predominated in the Westcity Project, within the Northcity Project a 'housing' culture prevailed. The project was delivered by the city council's Housing Solutions Service but also sat within the authority's Anti-Social Behaviour and Homelessness Strategies. Members of project staff were from a range of professional backgrounds but predominantly from housing-related services, including ASB teams, housing management, tenancy support workers and homelessness officers. The Project Manager suspected that it was the influence of her professional background in housing management that led her to recruit staff with experience of working within the housing sector and view them as being suitable for the post.

It became apparent through interviews with staff, that the knowledge base and professional values/culture of the staff shaped the project in key ways. The project was described as one that was committed to the use of enforcement measures where necessary for the purpose of protecting the wider community. This was made clear in the project's publicity material in which it was stated that the project staff would use enforcement measures where appropriate to 'motivate' families to change. The Project Manager explicitly contrasted this approach to one adopted by those FIPs that were ideologically situated within social care or operating with the independent sector whereby the focus of the project was perceived to be the family rather than the wider community. Furthermore, the Project Manager explained that her desire to manage the Northcity Project was driven by what she perceived as the failure of other agencies to deal adequately with families accused of causing ASB. She felt that other agencies had been too lenient in their attempts to work with such families and that a more 'assertive' approach was required – one that recognised the rights of the victims and 'challenged' the family rather than 'just hold their hand'.

Key workers described how the approach to their work with families was founded on the development of trusting relationships. They placed great importance on persevering with families, and being caring, honest, respectful and consistent in their dealings with them. For families, the approach that key workers took was experienced, largely, as non-stigmatising and sensitive, and for the women interviewed, in most cases, this 'befriending' role was valued and important in improving their quality of life (Parr 2011). Yet a key difference between the Westcity and the Northcity Projects was the latter's commitment to the use of punitive measures on the grounds of non-compliance, which was stated as being a defining feature of the project. Indeed, key workers spelled out to families the consequences that may befall them should they fail to meet their side of the support plan agreement. Key workers used the threat of enforcement and sanction more readily, and it was more central to their ideology. However, it was evident that there was a fundamental contradiction between the role of the project workers as 'help-givers' and agents responsible for enforcing compliance with tenancy agreements and other legal tools such as antisocial behaviour orders (ASBOs) (Parr 2011). 'Support' backed up by 'enforcement' is not always conducive to positive change.

Professional habitus also seemed to be a key influencing factor in the ways in which families needs were identified, understood and responded to. As was the case with the Westcity Project, support workers in the Northcity Project aimed to work holistically with families and use their professional judgement about an appropriate response to their assessment of a family's needs. In the Northcity Project however, it was common for interviewees to talk of 'parenting' together with the establishment of routines as being the primary problem in all families that required intervention. Related to this, since most of the project staff were from a housing background, few had experience, qualifications or training in providing social care and therapeutic support to families with high-level needs. This appeared to limit what the project workers were able to offer families, particularly in terms of the direct, one-to-one intervention provided, and therefore narrowed the focus of the intervention. In terms of direct support and reflecting the role of key workers in other projects (Batty and Flint 2012; Flint et al. 2011), their role was about emotional (e.g. one-to-one chats), financial assistance (taking up benefit entitlement, managing money) and practical help. The latter was a core part of the project's intervention and was centred on parenting 'education' and practical household management. Key workers in the Northcity Project acted more as (or perhaps more accurately were more comfortable acting as) facilitators and their role was concerned with advocating for the family and referring on to other services. Thus, dealing with the consequences of, for instance, domestic violence, which was acknowledged as prevalent among nearly all families referred, did not feature in the remit of key workers, while being acknowledged as having had deleterious consequences for families. These workers were not specialist providers in the way that project workers in the Westcity Project might be described. It might also be due to their lack of experience in working with families with high level needs that some project workers struggled to maintain professional boundaries such that families had become very emotionally attached to them, and dependency was an issue.

As a result of the project workers' more limited experience in support work and knowledge of policy and practice in that arena, the project's relationship with the local children's social work services was complex. The latter provided support to the project with the Social Care Manager sitting on the steering group and attending admissions panel meetings, for instance, and was described as its most influential partner. The incentives for social services to establish a partnership with Northcity Project were made clear during an interview with the Social Services Manager. He explained that in the political context, social services had insufficient resources, which limited the number of families they could support at any one time. He also drew attention to the way in which this had worked to narrow social services' focus to the single issue of child protection. Moreover, the amount of time social workers could devote to monitoring and assessing the safety of a child was limited, meaning that enforcement action was sometimes taken as a precautionary step. In this context, the Northcity Project was described as providing an additional resource for social services. The Social Services Manager suggested that had the Northcity Project not been involved with some families, social workers might well have been compelled to take more intrusive and punitive measures through a childcare route. Project workers were described as providing an additional 'plank of monitoring' and they, in comparison to social workers, could spend more time immersed in the families' lives observing them and could alert social services to any child protection concerns they identified.

The Social Work Manager and the local authority Lead Officer acknowledged that the agendas of social services and the project had come into conflict in the beginning, as social services attempted to appropriate the service for their own purposes – to refer cases to the project in order to allow social workers to withdraw contact or facilitate additional surveillance. This caused problems, not least because the complexity of the cases was beyond the ability of project staff, most untrained in social care, to deal with them. Although it was felt that this tension had been resolved to a degree through more careful referral and admissions procedures, a feeling prevailed that the Northcity Project was still acting as an additional arm of social services. Where social workers were providing a non-statutory service, there was a view amongst project staff that social services were often keen to withdraw their support completely due to the pressures of high case loads and limited resources. In other cases, where social services had a statutory responsibility to retain involvement, project workers suggested that social workers tended to visit less frequently with the assurance that monitoring was being carried out by project staff. This meant that project workers were effectively left providing (unqualified) social work support to families: 'We're just a cheaper alternative to social services.' Indeed, the salaries of these FIWs were significantly lower than those paid to support workers in the Westcity Project.

Although key workers were aware of their limitations and felt uncomfortable undertaking what they perceived to be the tasks of social workers, the fact that they were unqualified was not considered to be a disadvantage for the project staff. The possession of a certain 'type' of personality and/or 'life experience' was theorised as being more important than the possession of a professional knowledge base or formal qualifications. It was felt that 'people skills', including the ability to be empathetic, patient and non-judgemental, as well as assertive, were paramount qualities that project workers required, rather than specific methods or ways of working. In turn, this meant that project practices were not generally informed by any theoretical or practice models. The label that was applied to the approach was one described as a 'common-sense approach'. The key workers' lack of training was a concern for some local partner agencies however, who emphasised the limits to what project workers were able to achieve and the associated need for other services to remain involved with a family and not place too much responsibility on project workers:

They're not social workers and I don't think they should have to take on that type of responsibility either. I think my biggest fear for anybody involved in these projects is that they'll become pseudo social workers and take on an awful lot of responsibility that really perhaps is outside their remit, and that will mean that other agencies may absolve themselves of that responsibility.

Discussion

The particular focus of this chapter has been on the occupational culture of key workers and the ways in which intensive family interventions differ as a result of the professional background of project staff and the prevailing ethos of the project. I have drawn on evidence that has emerged as part of two larger pieces of research.

It is important to note that in both projects, key workers expressed a strong commitment to the families they supported, their intentions were clearly benevolent and they wanted to help families achieve positive change. Moreover, staff in both projects seemed to possess the necessary skills to carry out the 'emotional labour' that is central to building good relationships in family support work (Mason 2012). This entailed working with a range of agencies that often had competing policy objectives and where relationships were politically infused. In so doing, they engaged in complex, nuanced practices in order to engage with families that had often been hard to engage in the past. However, while the skill that this relationship-based work entails should be recognised and commended, questions must be asked about the equally important issue of the role of expertise, professional values, quality, training and accountability if we are to develop our understanding of how these projects work to best benefit families (Jones 2012).

The limited evidence we have suggests that occupational identities and a professional culture of key workers has a significant impact on the way families' needs are assessed and responded to (Parr 2008, 2007). For instance, the evidence indicates the following:

- Professionally and less qualified key workers might prioritise different needs in their assessments and diagnoses of a family needs.

- Professionally qualified key workers are able to provide specialist one-to-one support, whereas less qualified workers tend to act more as 'facilitators' with their role primarily concerned with advocating for the family and referring on to other services.

- The level of experience and background of the key worker is likely to impact on the extent to which they operate autonomously and assist or coordinate the work of other services.

- Qualification and training impacts on the extent to which FIWs can secure the 'buy-in' of other professionals.

- Key workers engage in duties that cross professional boundaries, and less qualified key workers can feel they are undertaking social work 'on the cheap'.

- Key workers can be used in ways that are beyond the expectations of formal policies and may lead to the exploitation of the FIW role.

- The emphasis placed on 'sanction' in motivating change is related to the cultural ethos and professional background of the service.

- 'Partner' agencies often commend the work of key workers but also express concern about the level of responsibility place on less qualified workers.

What does this mean for where the key worker role is positioned in relation to social work? Indeed, key workers undertake tasks and functions that may once have been (or still are) the preserve of social workers. Key workers are required to collate and process complex (sometimes competing) information about people and their lives and take appropriate courses of action to help them bring about change. The professional competences and the intellectual capital that a trained professional such as a social worker might bring to the role should perhaps not be underestimated:

> Gathering, sifting and determining the significance of disparate information in making judgements and drawing on social work's knowledge-base in promoting evidence-informed practice set within the context of experience-based practice wisdom require the intellectually rigorous application of critical appraisal skills and a competence in communication to be able to engage with and influence others. (Jones 2012, p.7)

What is more, where key workers are qualified social workers or work to shared occupational standards and competencies as social workers, they could potentially allow social workers a space for meaningful relationship-based work in which they can enjoy greater scope and flexibility to work with families (Mason 2012; Parr 2008; Parr 2012). Garrett has directed scepticism at such a suggestion, arguing that family intervention work is in fact deeply ideological and part of a wider project in which the language of radical social work has been co-opted into neoliberal processes (Garrett 2012). In the context of scarce resources and a discernible shift in the official language around family support, vigilance around the promotion of 'creativity' is important. However, rather than finding reasons why such interventions are destined to fail (Matthews 2009), as Rogowski (2012) has pointed out, we must look at how theoretical calls for a different kind of social work can be put into practice – how alternatives can be realised. It is not impossible that intensive family intervention could be used to re-enchant social work. Without wishing to romanticise such projects, social workers may be able to take these opportunities to engage in progressive practice.

If, however, intensive family interventions are managed and staffed by teams with little or no social work (or allied) experience, care needs to be taken in ensuring that the demands placed on unqualified and inexperienced staff are not unduly high, that appropriate training is provided and that close liaison is maintained with social workers such that cases where there are child protection concerns are addressed in partnership. Key workers can potentially support the work of lead social workers and fill a gap in service provision that currently exists. There is a long history of (non-qualified) Family Support Workers and Social Work Assistants being employed in social work. Yet sessional workers and Social Work Assistants often work alongside lead social workers and carry out routine tasks. Key workers, by contrast, often act more autonomously without formal links with social workers and undertake more complex work. It is not the case therefore that there is not a role for key workers untrained in social work and non-professionally educated, but that their role needs to be clearly defined together with their relationships with other agencies – particularly social workers whose core tasks and functions most closely resemble those of key workers. It may be that the key worker role becomes more about facilitating and coordinating agency involvement and providing emotional, practical and financial support but less about providing specialist support directly (Flint *et al.* 2011). However, questions remain about the extent to which an emerging professional occupation is guided by a particular professional ideology and is underpinned by a specific body of knowledge and underlying value and a knowledge base of support. The relationship between key workers and social work could produce a productive working partnership; alternatively, the two occupations could find themselves in conflict with each other (Scourfield 2010).

There is a risk, however, that projects offer social work 'on the cheap' as the above discussion suggests. The families referred to FIPs have complex and multiple needs and there needs to be an assurance that they are being supported by professionals appropriately trained to deal with the complexities they may face. This reflects a wider concern regarding the the fact that the number of non-professional caring occupations is expanding more rapidly than any other type of occupation (Cameron 2010). Carey (2006) has drawn attention to what he calls the 'darker side of unqualified social work', which he describes as a transient and low-paid sector. Without wanting to undermine the much-valued flexibility and creativity inherent within the key worker role, the absence of professional association and regulation could create a context in which there is a need for some standardisation of practice with underpinning values and competencies, together with a code of practice (Jones 2012). Where key workers may work quite independently, there is also a question of where it leaves families in terms of protection against bad practice, their rights to complain and issues of accountability and quality assurance more generally. While, one model or approach might not be desirable and projects need to respond to local need, para-professions and newly emerging roles within the field of social care, it perhaps needs to not be so vaguely defined and unregulated (Cameron 2010; Scourfield 2010).

Conclusion

The question of who is best qualified to do family support work is difficult to answer. It is my intention that the discussion here adds to the growing body of evidence that is furnishing our understanding of the different ways FIPs 'work' within different contexts. This chapter is just a beginning, however. Unpicking exactly how professional ideology manifests itself in practice and the substance of the intervention requires more research. There is a pressing need for detailed sociological studies of 'who works' in family support with a focus on key workers' backgrounds, training, values and beliefs, as well as family intervention occupational cultures more generally.

References

Batty, E., and Flint, J. (2012) 'Conceptualising the contexts, mechanisms and outcomes of intensive family intervention projects.' *Social Policy and Society* *11*, 3, 345–358.

Batty, E., Crisp, R., Green, S., Platts-Fowler, D. and Robinson, D. (2013) *Key Working and Whole Household Interventions in Sheffield: Key Lessons and Priorities for Action*. Sheffield: CRESR/Sheffield City Council.

Cameron, A. (2010) 'The contribution of housing support workers to joined up services.' *Journal of Interprofessional Care 24*, 1, 100–10.

Carey, M. (2006) 'Everything must go? The privatisation of State social work.' *British Journal of Social Work*, doi: 10.1093/bjsw/bcl373.

Children's Workforce Development Council (2011) *Providing Intense Support for Families with Multiple and Complex Needs*. Leeds: Children's Workforce Development Council.

Children's Workforce Development Council (2012) *Parenting Workforce Analysis*. Leeds: Children's Workforce Development Council.

Department for Communities and Local Government (2012) *Working with Troubled Families: A Guide to the Evidence and Good Practice*. London: Department for Communities and Local Government.

Flint, J., Batty, E., Parr, S., Platts-Fowler, D., Nixon, J. and Sanderson, D. (2011) *Evaluation of Intensive Intervention Projects*. London: Department for Education.

Garrett, P.M. (2012) 'Re-enchanting social work? The emerging "spirit" of social work in an age of economic crisis.' *British Journal of Social Work 44*, 3, 503–521.

Hayden, C. and Jenkins, C. (2013) 'Children taken into care and custody and the "troubled families" agenda in England.' *Child and Family Social Work*. Available at http://onlinelibrary.wiley.com/doi/10.1111/cfs.12095/abstract, accessed on 11 October 2014.

Jones, R. (2012) 'The best of times, the worst of times: social work and its moment.' *British Journal of Social Work 44*, 3, 485–502.

Mason, C. (2012) 'Social work and the "art of relationship": parents' perspectives on an intensive family support project.' *Child and Family Social Work 17*, 368–377.

Matthews, R. (2009) 'Beyond "so what?" criminology.' *Theoretical Criminology 13*, 3, 341–362.

Natcen (National Centre for Social Research) (2010) *Antisocial Behaviour Family Intervention Projects: Monitoring and Evaluation*. London: Department for Children, Schools and Famlies.

Nixon, J., Hunter, C., Parr, S., Myers, S., Whittle, S. and Sanderson, D. (2006) *Anti-Social Behaviour Intensive Family Support Projects: An Evaluation of Six Pioneering Projects*. London: ODPM.

Parr, S. (2007) *The Leeds Signpost Family Intervention Project: An Evaluation*. Sheffield: CRESR, Sheffield Hallam University.

Parr, S. (2008) 'Family intervention projects: a site of social work practice.' *British Journal of Social Work*. Available at http://bjsw.oxfordjournals.org/content/39/7/1256.abstract, accessed on 12 October 2014.

Parr, S. (2011) 'Family policy and the governance of anti-social behaviour in the UK: women's experiences of intensive family support.' *Journal of Social Policy 40*, 4, 717–737.

Parr, S. (2012) 'Intensive family casework with 'problem families': past and present.' *Family Science 2*, 4, 240–249.

Prior, D. (2007) *Continuities and Discontinuities in Governing Anti-Social Behaviour*. Birmingham: University of Birmingham.

Respect Task Force (2006) *Respect Action Plan*. London: Home Office.

Rogowski, S. (2012) 'Social work with children and families: challenges and possibilities in the neo-liberal world.' *British Journal of Social Work 42*, 5, 921–940.

Scourfield, P. (2010) 'Going for brokerage: a task of "independent support" or social work?' *British Journal of Social Work 40*, 858–877.

Stenson, K. (2005) 'Sovereignity, biopolitics and the local government of crime in Britain.' *Theoretical Criminology 9*, 3, 265–287.

White, C., Warrener, M., Reeves, A. and LaValle, I. (2008) *Family Intervention Projects: An Evaluation of their Design, Set-up and Early Outcomes.* London: Department for Children, Schools and Families.

CHAPTER 4

The 'Family Recovery' Approach to Helping Struggling Families

PROFESSOR JUNE THOBURN,
UNIVERSITY OF EAST ANGLIA

Introduction

Towards the tail end of the Labour Government, as the evaluations of the Family Intervention Projects (FIPs) began to appear (Cabinet Office, Social Exclusion Task Force 2008), there was a realisation that some of the most vulnerable families, especially those with younger children, were not being included in the intensive intervention projects. This is unsurprising, since much of the impetus for rolling out the FIPs came from concerns about 'nuisance neighbours' and anti-social behaviour (ASB) of teenagers. One result was that these services for 'troublesome families' were as likely to be sited (especially in non-unitary local authorities) in housing or community safety teams as in children's services teams (Thoburn 2013). The interdepartmental report *Aiming High for Children: Supporting Families* (HM Treasury and Department for Children, Schools and Families (DCSF) 2007, p.61) pointed to concerns about the rising numbers of children in all age groups in need of child protection services or 'on the edge of care'. In response, central Government funding was made available for a pathfinder programme 'to test ways of providing more effective support to families at risk' (DCSF 2010, p.1).

Westminster children's services department was already the lead agency providing a FIP service in the borough, and it recognised the potential presented by the pathfinder funding to broaden its intensive intervention service to families where there were child protection concerns. Central Government funded an evaluation of all 15 of the Think Family pathfinders (Kendall, Rodger and Palmer 2010; York Consulting 2011). However, the Westminster Children's social services senior managers commissioned the UEA Centre for Research on Children and Families to provide a more detailed process evaluation of their Family Recovery Project (FRP) and to make recommendations about long-term sustainability and integration with their services as usual.

The Family Recovery Project

As required by the Government tendering process, the Westminster FRP took on board many of the working practices and lessons learned from the existing FIPs. Key characteristics shared by FIPs and the Think Family projects were:

- meeting the needs of individual family members within a whole family approach
- the allocation of an Intensive Outreach Worker (IOW)
- a case plan agreed with the parents and older children spelling out the 'rewards' when goals were achieved and the likely consequences if they were not.

There were, however, characteristics specific to the Westminster FRP shared with only a minority of the other pilots.

- The multidisciplinary service was led by a senior Children's Social Work Manager and the dominant 'ethos' was a social work one.
- High value was placed on the specialist contribution (to the work with individual families and of the project as a whole) of team members drawn from across adult and children's social care, primary and specialist physical and

mental health and addictions services, education, housing, community safety (including specialists with expertise with victims and perpetrators of domestic abuse), welfare rights/debt counselling and a preparation for employment specialist.

- The team was located alongside child protection and locality teams, facilitating continuity of service before, during and after the FRP service.

- The information analyst section (including police officers seconded to the team), with the permission of parents accepting the offer of the service, compiled and updated information from all relevant sources.

Two major differences from the other FIP and Think Family projects were as follows.

- Day-to-day work with the family was shared between two lead professionals – an FRP IOW and a lead worker for the child/ren (not a member of the specialist FRP team and usually a social worker from one of the children's services teams).

- 'Team Around the Family' (TAF) meetings chaired by the team manager responsible for casework supervision of the lead IOW were held approximately every three weeks for the professional network and every six weeks with family members.

Box 1 lists the full- and part-time members of the team. Most were employed by children's social services but some were seconded by the education, housing or adult social services departments of the local authority, the voluntary sector, police or health services.

Box 1: Members of the Westminster FRP team (some part-time)

- FRP team manager (senior children's services social worker)

- two assistant team managers (senior social workers)
- eight full-time equivalent IOWs (varied educational and professional backgrounds and relevant experience)
- business manager and clerical support
- information scientist/data analyst
- adult mental health social worker
- two domestic violence specialist workers
- addictions specialist social worker
- health visitor
- welfare benefits adviser (part-time secondment from a Family Centre)
- teacher in role of school link worker
- housing advice worker.

The research aims and methods

The research had both evaluative and descriptive components. This dual approach facilitated an understanding of the processes and practice of the team and enabled the researchers to make a contribution to service planning both during the research period and at the end of the 'pathfinder' stage of the work.

The broadly ethnographic research approach adopted for the observational study of team interactions and decision-making on individual cases (Broadhurst *et al.* 2009) was facilitated by the open-plan working environment. Two members of the research team spent time collecting data from electronic records, observing interactions between team members and conducting opportunistic as well as scheduled interviews with team members.

Basic demographic data (already collected for the national evaluation) were available on all families referred in the first year and analysed with respect to the first 100 completed cases (accepted for a service between February 2009 and July 2010). This quantitative element also linked into the economic analysis, which also drew on reports for senior managers provided by the FRP team. Committee reports, monitoring data and internal evaluation reports were also available to the researchers.

Data on the full cohort of the first 100 completed cases were complemented by a detailed process analysis of the work with a purposive sample of 33 families (a one-third sample), Process and interim outcome data were analysed from information systematically extracted from case records. These were complemented by qualitative data from interviews with managers and caseworkers, attendance at team meetings and observation of TAF and professionals' meetings.

We did not set out to gain systematically the views of parents or children and were reliant on information about their satisfaction or otherwise with the service on records of family meetings and on the small number of conversations before and after meetings they and we attended. In this respect, and also with respect to the views of the TAF members from other agencies, our findings are complemented by the research of Ray Jones (see Chapter 6) who found a high level of satisfaction of both parents and colleagues with the work of Wandsworth FRP, which adopted a very similar approach.

'Researcher rating' protocols were developed for analysis (e.g. grouping types of families, levels of seriousness of problems, patterns of service delivery, approaches to helping and interim outcomes for parents and children). Additional detail on the research methodology is available from Thoburn *et al.* (2010a) and Thoburn *et al.* (2011, 2013).

The families

The target group for the Think Family pathfinders was families with multiple and complex difficulties 'caught in a cycle of low achievement including those who are not being effectively engaged and supported by existing services' (Department for Education (DCSF) 2010, p.2). As the project developed, the FRP began to prioritise families where complexity of difficulties was also linked with a high risk of statutory intervention by children's social care services because a child was in need of a protective service or 'on the edge of care'. Between October 2008 and the end of April 2011 306 families were referred to the project. Of these, 135 (44%) were offered a service; 121 took up the offer and 14 decided not to take it up. In total, 167 (56%) were considered not to meet the threshold for a FRP service. This chapter focuses on the full cohort of the first 100 completed cases and the 'intensive sample' of 33 families who were broadly representative of those accepted for a service.

Somewhat contrary to what was anticipated by those framing the policy, very young parents did not figure highly. The average age of mothers in the full cohort was 40, with a range from 20 to 59 years. Unsurprisingly, since 'complexity' was a reason for referral, there were more families with three or more children in the household than in the general population. A large minority had children in different age groups, including some adult 'children' still in the household or living nearby. Some of the fathers had children from a previous relationship, and some children were in care or had been adopted. There were fewer 'reconstituted families' than is often the case with families referred to children's services; this was probably related to the large population of first or second generation immigrant families from ethnic groups where marriage breakdown is less frequent. However, some mothers and more fathers had previous children by different partners, and this could have contributed to ongoing emotional stress, especially if the earlier relationship had involved domestic abuse. Data on the ethnicity of the mothers was missing for 26 of the 100 cohort families (even more so for fathers) but where this was available, 22 were recorded as 'White British' and 51 different minority ethnicities were recorded for either mothers or fathers in the remaining 52 families. Twenty mothers were described as having some difficulty with spoken and/or written English.

Information on drug and alcohol abuse (identified with respect to about a quarter of the families) and criminality (at some point there had been police involvement with 75% of the families) appeared to be accurately recorded for the whole sample. From our more detailed information on the small sample families, it was clear that mental health and physical health problems were under-recognised at the time of referral, At least 60 per cent of the parents in the small sample households had a problem with mental ill-health (mostly not formally diagnosed or treated only at primary health care level). In 1 in 5 of the 33 small sample families a parent had a physical health problem or disability and this was the case with respect of at least one child in a third of the families.

Table 4.1 Cases where there were child protection concerns (small sample: more than one answer possible)

Concern	Number of families	%
Parenting deficits	30	91
Child at risk of statutory protective intervention	29	88
Improve safeguarding an aim of intervention	22	67
Concerns about neglect	22	67
Reducing impact of domestic abuse is an aim of intervention	14	42
Child on Child Protection Plan at referral to FRP or during case	11	33
Child protection team social worker was lead professional for child or member of TAF	9	27

With respect to child safeguarding issues, Table 4.1 shows (for the small sample cases where data were more reliable) aspects of the life of at least one child in the family that was a cause for concern or where there had been a formal child protection intervention.

Some of the families could be described as 'hard to reach' and whilst some had sought help, they had acquired the label of 'hard to change' (Thoburn 2010b). In the case records of families known to agencies for some years (usually provided with a short-term service at times of crisis) it was not uncommon to find the words 'uncooperative', 'oppositional' and 'false compliance'. However, we found support in the case records for the hypothesis of Daniel *et al.*

(2011, p.58) that the label 'hard to reach' may conceal a service delivery problem: a problem that was recognised by the FRP service planners and practitioners. Using groupings first devised by researchers whose studies were reported in the *Child Protection: Messages from Research* overview (Department of Health 1995) and since adapted to categorise reasons for children entering care, the proportion of families in this sample with long-term and multiple difficulties (33%) was slightly lower than the 40 per cent in the 'significant harm' cohort of Brandon and Thoburn (2008) and there were more 'specific issues' families. However there were very few with one 'single issue', demonstrating the complexity of these families accepted for an FRP service, even when compared with a 'confirmed' significant harm cohort.

The components of the FRP service

Although the route to a FRP service often started with a community-based 'tier 2' professional, the actual referral was in most cases made by a children's services duty or locality team social worker. The triggers for referral were an assessment that a child was 'on the edge of care' or there were child protection concerns, but also that there were indications that at least one parent recognised that the family was at a turning point and might be willing to accept the flexible but intensive service offered by the FRP team. Following screening by the FRP management team, an IOW talked with the parents (almost always in the family home) about the services and support that might be provided, what the family hoped to achieve and the changes that the agencies considered necessary if more coercive actions to secure children's wellbeing were to be avoided. Although, as with the FIPs, community and neighbourhood concerns were addressed, the emphasis was on family relationships and child wellbeing concerns. During this visit there was discussion about which professionals would be included in the TAF and agreement had to be reached for the sharing of information (on a 'need to know' basis), amongst all those working with family members before the referral could proceed. An outline agreement for the first phase of the FRP service was signed by the IOW and the parent/s. This was elaborated on at a meeting of all the professionals currently involved with the family (sometimes attended by parents and older children) at which the smaller TAF and the two lead professionals were identified.

There was always one FRP outreach worker (and sometimes two) providing flexible services to the family as a whole and, as appropriate, to parents and children as individuals. The safety and welfare of each child was always at the forefront, but beyond that the decisions about how best to help and the priorities for the issues to be tackled were for the parents, older children and workers to agree on. That said, the usual pattern for the first stage was for there to be two or more IOW home visits a week. At a later stage the IOW might go with a parent to a health service or housing appointment or a meeting with a teacher or join family members in a leisure activity. The second lead professional was usually the children's services or adolescent team social worker who already knew the family. Their role was to be alert to any child safeguarding issues but also to share in the casework with the family.

The approach to multidisciplinary teamwork was that these two lead professionals would draw on the skills and specialist expertise of their colleagues as needed and agreed with the family members. Sometimes this meant that the specialist worker acted as a consultant to the IOW, at other times they worked jointly and at other times a specialist took on an agreed short-term piece of work, such as helping a parent to sort out debts or going with a parent to school to plan the re-entry of an excluded child. A particularly important role for adult social care or health specialists was to advocate for a parent to receive a specialist primary care or specialist service. This might have been refused in the past because, although essential to improvements in the family, the parent had been assessed as 'not meeting the threshold'.

Central to this approach was that the service provided varied according to the needs, wishes and capabilities of the family members and that it changed as circumstances changed. The three weekly professionals' meetings and the six weekly TAF meetings involving the parents and older children were opportunities to review progress and agree any changes to the case plan. Although costly, these were considered essential to ensure that the service remained focused. It was these meetings that decided the case might be closed to FRP and the components of the follow-up services.

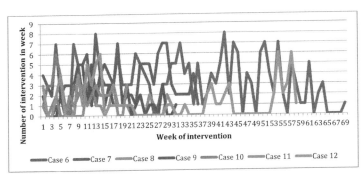

FIGURE 4.1 PATTERN OF SERVICE INTENSITY AND DURATION FOR THE 7 CASES USED IN THE COST ANALYSIS

Figure 4.1 illustrates (with respect to seven of the families) the flexibility in service intensity and duration. Leaving aside the small number that closed quickly because a family withdrew or a family moved out of the borough, duration ranged from 4 to 18 months, with the mean being 7 months. It is the flexibility in terms of service components, casework approaches and case duration that marks the FRP out from most earlier intensive family preservation approaches and some of the 'manualised', 'evidence-based' programmes being piloted at the same time (e.g. multi-systematic therapy [MST] and Functional Family Therapy), which share some of the same characteristics.

The emphasis in the first phase was usually on practical services to tackle the presenting problems that had led the family members to accept the service. Most often this involved assistance with debts, housing problems, school issues and help to access appropriate physical or mental health care or an addictions treatment service. Immediate problems of domestic abuse had usually been at least temporarily resolved before the FRP case opened, but a domestic abuse worker focusing on the impact of past abuse on (usually) the mother was often a key TAF member.

Boxes 2 and 3 give examples of the teams around the 'J' family (a longer term, higher cost case) and the 'O' 'family (a shorter duration, high-intensity, lower cost case). (Some details have been changes to protect confidentiality.)

Box 2: The 'J' family

Mr and Mrs J are long-term White British residents of the borough. At the time of referral, the five children still in the household were aged between 2 and 17. Mr J was the father of the youngest two children but not the eldest three boys, who saw their own father spasmodically. Each parent had adult children who were sometimes also resident. Both Mr and Mrs J had mental health difficulties. For Mr J this was exacerbated by cannabis usage. Mrs J had suffered serious domestic abuse in her previous relationship.

The school had made a referral to children's social services (with the agreement of the parents) when they were told that the 12-year-old had been 'going missing' from home and sleeping rough. When at school he was either withdrawn or occasionally had an outburst of temper, which had resulted in temporary exclusions. The youngest two children were described as 'under-stimulated' and the family was described as 'at times chaotic' but the parents were also said to be able to provide emotional warmth when not overwhelmed by their own problems.

Mr J was mostly in receipt of benefits but he and the 17-year-old were sometimes in part-time work. Mrs J was not seeking work because of the age of the children. The family income was low and irregular; there were debts, and eviction from their council accommodation was threatened (together with the school exclusion, the precipitating reason for the FRP referral).

Figure 4.2 illustrates the J family's TAF, of which there were eight members. From the (inner circle) FRP team, the IOW was supported at some point by the addictions specialist, the adult mental health social worker, the benefits adviser and the domestic violence counsellor. Also involved (the 'outer circle') were the locality team social worker (lead professional for the children) the community health visitor and the psychologist from the adult mental health team. The children's headteachers sometimes attend TAF meetings and the IOW and locality social worker were in regular contact with them.

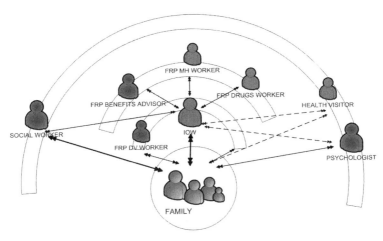

FIGURE 4.2 J FAMILY 'TAF' APPROXIMATELY HALF
FRP AND HALF OUTSIDE AGENCIES

The IOW was the lead professional for parents but provided a range of supports in the home and community for all family members. She provided a relationship-based supportive casework service to Mrs J into which she introduced aspects of one of the well-known parenting programmes in which she had been trained. The FRP domestic violence specialist provided a counselling service to the mother, focused on trauma from earlier domestic violence and practical help in arranging safe contact between the oldest children and their father. Because the family had been overwhelmed by too many workers in the past, the IOW initially received advice from the FRP specialist drugs worker, mental health social worker and welfare benefits worker (debt counselling). Later on, joint visits or individual sessions were arranged. The mental health worker liaised with the parents' GP and arranged a mental health assessment for the father, resulting in a short-term service from the psychologist, to assist in reducing his use of cannabis, followed by regular monitoring by the mental health social worker of his prescribed medication. The locality team social worker and the IOW worked jointly with the 12-year-old, liaising closely with the school and arranging leisure and sporting activities.

After 13 months, it was agreed by the team members and by Mr and Mrs J that they were all benefitting from the routine introduced into the home, and the stress levels were reduced because the threat of eviction had been lifted and they were managing to reduce other debts. The oldest child was now in receipt of income support and was on a work preparation scheme. At case closure to FRP, the key worker was the locality social worker. Mrs J was a regular attender at the Family Centre with her youngest child. She also accessed the counselling service at the centre and a counsellor attached to the surgery monitored her prescribed medication.

Box 3: The 'O' family

The case of Ms O is an example of a shorter duration, high-intensity service – mainly provided by the FRP IOW with support from FRP specialists. At referral, Ms O (a second generation immigrant of Pakistani heritage) had sought police assistance to have a physically abusive partner (the father of her children aged three and 18 months) removed from her home and had obtained a court injunction. She was living in unsatisfactory and insecure privately rented accommodation. She suffered from depression and a growing dependence on prescription drugs was resulting in tiredness and lethargy, which was impacting on the children. The health visitor referred the family to children's services because she considered that they were being emotionally neglected. The home was described as 'chaotic' with poor standards of cleanliness. Ms O was also worried about debts and had still not fully sorted out post-separation financial and child contact arrangements.

In the context of a supportive relationship, the IOW focused her work on creating routines and a more ordered home environment and providing practical advice on parenting. She also introduced Ms O to the family centre, going with her until she felt comfortable on her own, and arranged a pre-school place for the three-year-old. She liaised with the FRP domestic violence worker about managing risk and addressing the impact of past abuse. The social worker (lead professional for the children) helped her to contact a solicitor to arrange appropriate contact arrangements. The FRP substance abuse worker became involved to assess and refer Ms O for appropriate services once the IOW had established a working relationship with her. The FRP health visitor assessed and advised on the children's health needs and the welfare benefits adviser assisted in regularising the child support arrangements and making debt repayment arrangements. A grant from a charity helped to make the home more comfortable but at the end of the service (after seven months), attempts to secure more appropriate housing had not been successful. The case remained open ('with a child in need plan') to the locality social worker for three months and was then closed to children's services, with ongoing support provided by the family centre.

Casework approaches and methods

The flexibility that was apparent in the pattern of service delivery was also a feature of the casework approaches and methods. Both the approach to casework with individual families and the overall approach of the team managers and members displayed the overarching characteristics described by practitioners and researchers as being most likely to engage families with complex difficulties in the process of change (Daniel *et al.* 2011; Featherstone, White and Morris 2014; Thoburn 2010b). These were:

- an empathic and supportive casework relationship

- clarity about what has to change *but* 'start where the client is', i.e. assume parents will know their family best so be respectful of their views about what is likely to help

- clarity about how paramount children's protection and welfare is and honesty about what might trigger a more coercive intervention

- demonstrating concern for parents as individuals and paying attention to their health needs and relationship issues

- a flexible combination of practical help, support, educative approaches and therapy.

As researchers, we observed many examples of a team culture in which managers and more experienced workers 'modelled' this essentially caring, respectful and relationship-based approach. The team room was itself a nurturing and facilitating environment: phones were not left ringing and other team members would pick up the phone of an absent colleague and show concern and provide immediate 'holding' advice to a family. An addictions specialist said:

> It overwhelmed me when I came here. All in one big room – just being able to walk over there and say 'I've just seen Bill – how are things with the family?' As a practitioner, it is much easier to know where things are going. And for the family too – how to guide the client through their journey.

With respect to the 'carrot and stick' approach highlighted by the Government funders, the preferred approach was to emphasise rewards (including rehousing or approaches to charitable trusts to pay off debts), but there was clarity about consequences if the quality of care of a child fell below what was acceptable. Table 4.2 lists the possible sanctions mentioned in the agreements for the small sample cases, but in only a quarter was there a heavy emphasis on these sanctions in the day-to-day work.

Table 4.2 Sanctions referred to in contract or care plan (cases do not total 33 as more than one sanction used in some cases)

Sanctions referred to	Number of cases	%
Child into/remaining in care	11	33
Formal CP plan initiated/remain (but no likelihood of care)	5	15
ASBO made/retained/youth court hearing	3	9
ASBO/court child and adult (criminal or truancy)	5	15
Eviction/not rehoused	5	15
Eviction plus child into care/CP	3	9
No sanctions referred to	5	15

The approach of the IOWs, can be broadly described as 'relationship-based helping' or 'psychosocial casework', owing much to strengths-based or ecological models of practice. It combined practical help (sometimes of an intensive nature including short-term, out-of-home care for a troubled teenager) with the emotional support that gave some parents, at later stages of the case, the confidence to seek specialist help with deeper psychological or relationship problems. There was evidence that in most cases it was 'therapeutic', even though it was unusual for any specific therapy method to be used. The focus on improving the quality of parenting resulted in the appropriate use of educative and 'modelling' approaches. An IOW said:

> There was an initial battle with the family centre – it was slow moving – the mother was resistant at first – she didn't want therapy. Now after we've developed the relationship we've reintroduced the idea of therapy and the mother wants things to improve.

However, the many pressing needs meant that parents didn't have the time, energy or motivation to give over to completing 'pure model' parenting programmes, even if the offer was for them to be delivered on a one-to-one basis in the family home. Some had tried them in the past and dropped out. So rather than using any one programme as designed by the originators, workers used some of the techniques as part of their broader casework approach. As a service manager put it:

> That is one of the strengths of this project – the flexibility of response – recognising that all families are different. And all the needs are different. We have to fit around them. Rather than them fit into a pre-set service.

In the course of interviews with the FRP lead professionals and case supervisors, and when scrutinising the case records, we looked for examples of any specific casework methods or approaches with a clear theoretical underpinning. Individual workers tended to use a preferred approach with all the families they worked with (about half using a broadly psychosocial approach and about half a more behavioural or social learning approach). However, case supervisors encouraged workers to fit their approach to the needs of the family and to vary it as the circumstances changed. A mental health specialist commented:

> That is the joy. So many different individuals with different background into the melting pot. It is all about the ethos. Facilitating the family's journey. So all those different approaches come together very well. Sometimes a specific programme or intervention is right for the family but that is part of a bigger mix. When I'm working with families, my different – whole gamut of skills, are used as needed – whether it is CBT or reflective.

Whatever the casework approach, advocacy and mediation skills (between parents in the household and previous partners, between parents and adolescents, and between family members and relatives or neighbours) figured prominently. A role that IOWs shared with the FRP specialist team members was that of 'interpreting' particular issues for parents and children to the community-based services and thus helping to build bridges for when the case closed to FRP. Sometimes this involved 'shuttle diplomacy' (to help ease a youngster back into school or ease tensions with neighbours, a previous partner or the landlord) and sometimes going with family members to help them to explain their situation. For family members who had been known to services for some period of time and had acquired the 'uncooperative' or 'aggressive' label, this could be particularly important. A specialist worker said:

> Their dad felt as if he had been abandoned by services over the years. I went to meet him there. This is one of the key differences, working with FRP, I went to meet him two or three times a week in his home – made a relationship with him.

An IOW said the following at a team meeting, and the referring professional present confirmed that it was the case:

> We had done something that hadn't been done before. There has been a redefinition of the family.

A reminder here is appropriate of the recommendation of Daniel *et al.* (2011) that 'policy initiatives aimed to improve engagement with "hard to reach" parents should be complemented by strategies to ensure that services are not "hard to access"'.

Did the FRP reach the families it aimed to help?

The information provided earlier about the characteristics of the families indicates that the Westminster FRP was providing a service to a group of families that fitted the aims of the originators of the Think Family pathfinder initiative. All except a small minority of the families (somewhere between five and ten of the first hundred) who accepted the offer of a FRP service were families with multiple and complex needs in which at least one child was suffering or likely to be exposed to maltreatment or suffer significant impairment to their development if family stresses were not alleviated. Using the definitions of 'statutory', and 'specialist' levels of need of the national pathfinder evaluators, around 90 per cent were in need of a 'statutory' service and fewer than 5 per cent came into the 'universal' or 'targeted' levels of need as compared with around 37 per cent and 30 per cent of the 15 Think Family pathfinders (York Consulting 2011).

Given the recognition that the establishment of a casework relationship that is empathic, honest and reliable is of central importance if family members are to be helped to make changes in their lives, it is relevant to ask whether at least one team member managed to establish a trusting relationship at least with one parent. Since, for the majority of the parents and older children there was a long history of non-engagement, it is not surprising that a trusting relationship with the 'main' parent was established in fewer than half the cases (n =15). In a further 12 cases there was evidence that parents recognised the concern of the workers (as demonstrated by their reliability, persistence and attention to practical problems) but researchers concluded that their trust in the worker was at best ambivalent. This was particularly the case with parents who had mental health difficulties or were unable to give up addictions or move away from abusive relationships. In 6 of the 33 cases, the persistent attempts of the workers failed to move the parents beyond very superficial engagement with the work. However, in some cases when parents did not engage, the IOWs became important people in the lives of children, opened up leisure opportunities for them or helped them into employment or training. Some of the younger ones became fond of their IOW and looked forward to their visits.

Although satisfaction of team members is not in itself an indicator of a successful programme, it is certainly instrumental in securing worker continuity, low sickness rates and team cohesion. Interviews with service managers, administrators, IOWs and specialist professionals demonstrated a high degree of clarity about service aims, roles and overall satisfaction.

> I loved it. It was an extraordinary experience. It was a real blessing to come and work here – away from silos – having the resource within FRP to work in a multi-disciplinary way. It set me up for the direction services are going in: working in a multi-disciplinary team (adult mental health specialist).

A welfare benefits adviser said:

> We've always had that link which has got stronger since I've been here. I've got to value working with social workers.

Was there evidence that the service to parents and children was effective?

The earlier FIP programmes on which the Think Family pilots were to some extent modelled, and even more so the Troubled Families initiative, were set up to achieve specific aims that can be more easily measured. Reporting on the effectiveness of the FRP service is more problematic since the aims of the FRP with respect to each family and the reasons why families engaged with the service differed. For example, since school attendance was not a problem in 18 of the 33 families, improved attendance (a key TFP aim) was not an aim to be achieved for 15 of the small sample FRP families. Another TFP aim, reduction of criminal behaviour or ASB, was not an issue to be addressed at the time of referral in 18 of the families. On the other hand, achieving the aim of reducing the impact of addiction or mental or physical ill-health on the children is less easily measureable. With respect to the TFP high priority aim of families in sustained employment, the ill-health of an important minority of the parents and children meant that even part-time employment was not a priority, at least during the period of engagement with FRP. The aim most likely to be achieved was improvements in material circumstances (improvements realised for three-quarters of the small sample families). As well as contributing to the quality of life of parents and children, practical improvements such as improved housing or debt reduction, usually resulted in a reduction of stress in the families and parents being more emotionally available to their children. Practical assistance in the first phase of the work was seen by families as evidence that the FRP team members were concerned with issues that mattered to them and contributed to a greater level of engagement with community-based professionals as well as the FRP team members. This willingness to engage with services continued for many of the families after case closure.

Improved school attendance and reduced ASB of children were more likely to be fully achieved than, for example, total cessation of parental drug or alcohol intake or reducing the impact of longstanding domestic abuse. The aims of improved working with agencies and enhancing parenting skills were each achieved at least partially in around 60 per cent of the cases.

Since the overarching aim of the FRP was to improve the safety and wellbeing of the children and prevent further impairment to their health or development, a researcher rating protocol was devised, taking account of information from all sources to identify any changes in the wellbeing of the parents and children. Additionally, irrespective of any change achieved, we considered whether there was evidence that the children were of at least average wellbeing at FRP case closure. Table 4.3 gives our conclusions (with ratings cross-checked by researchers) with respect to the small sample families. Despite improvements in the wellbeing of at least one child in around 57 per cent of families (and deterioration in wellbeing for all the children in only one case and mixed results in in only four families), in only 39 per cent of the families could the wellbeing of all the children be described as at least 'average' (when compared with a child of a similar ability level or with a similar disability in a similar economic group). This was recognised in the arrangements for case closure in that only around a quarter of the families were no longer receiving a 'specialist' or 'statutory' service either from children's services teams or the youth justice services when the case closed to FRP.

Table 4.3 Interim outcome: overall wellbeing of child/ren (researcher rating)

Overall wellbeing	Number of cases	%
All below average	13	39
One/some below average – one/some average	10	30
All average	10	30

Keeping children out of care – an aim sometimes ascribed to such programmes – could lead to perverse incentives, since a well-managed entry into care with clear short- or long-term care plans to promote the child's wellbeing (as happened for a least one child in four of the cases in the one-third sub-sample cases) may lead to a positive long-term outcome. Similarly, the proportion of families no longer needing targeted or specialist support services is an inappropriate indicator of success: a more positive attitude to engagement with the services that are still needed is a more appropriate indicator, though more difficult to measure than no longer 'being on the books'. At the point of case closure with FRP, all except one of the families in the one-third sample had a plan for social work (in 26 of the 33 cases) or other specialist services to continue. The FRP service approach, which involved TAF members from community-based services, ensured that in most cases there was continuity of relationship with at least one TAF member after the intensive FRP service ended.

Table 4.4 Overall interim outcome for family following FRP service (researcher rating)

Interim outcome for family	Number of cases	%
Unsuccessful: no change in wellbeing of adults or children	4	12
Some aims achieved, still serious problems, family not accessing help	4	12
Some aims achieved still serious problems, family accessing help	4	12
Some aims achieved, still some problems, family accessing help	7	21
Successful: most aims achieved – still some problems, family managing/accessing help/ likely to seek timely help in future	8	24
Successful: aims mainly achieved, family managing well, children's wellbeing satisfactory	2	6
Still serious problems but FRP service helped to achieve a coherent case plan to improve wellbeing	4	12

Given the high level of vulnerability and the comparatively short duration of the FRP service, it is no surprise that even though in most cases some aims were achieved, only around a third could be rated as having achieved a 'successful' overall outcome at the time of case closure. Table 4.4 shows that on a global rating of the interim outcomes, taking account of all sources of information available, we concluded that at the time of case closure in around 63 per cent of the small sample families sustainable improvements in wellbeing had been achieved for most of the family members, including the youngest children. In a further four cases, the work of the FRP resulted in clarification of a complex situation allowing a clear plan to be made for safeguarding and promoting the welfare of some very vulnerable children by a well-planned and sensitively managed placement in care. Only four of the small sample cases (an estimate of around 12% of the total accepted for a service) were rated as unsuccessful in that no positive change was achieved or there was deterioration in the general functioning of the family, with a further four at risk of slipping back because they were not accessing appropriate services at case closure.

Our predictions were that: around half of the families would need a long-term lower intensity or episodic service from a specialist service catering for the needs of vulnerable families (a children's social services locality or adolescents team or a neighbourhood family centre with some social work input); around a quarter would need a more intensive service for at least a period; in around 15 per cent of cases children would need an out-of-home care service or a child or young adult would be subject to a custodial sentence.

An important caveat to this section on interim outcomes is that since there was no control or even comparison group, it is not possible to say that the service 'caused' any improvement; only that any improvement or deterioration that occurred did so over the period when the service was being provided.

Conclusions and comparisons with the FIP and TFP

On the surface, these findings appear less positive than those reported by the FIP and Troubled Families evaluators. However, the Think Families initiative specifically targeted families with complex difficulties where children were at serious risk of needing a formal child protection intervention or out-of-home placement. I would argue from a reading of the available evaluations that the triggers for inclusion in the FIP and the TFP and, for the latter, the stated aims and the specified results that triggered payment, have the effect of providing the service to more 'troublesome' and fewer really 'troubled' families (those at serious risk of long-term family breakdown or separation) than was the case with the FRP service (Thoburn 2013). The evidence from the FRP evaluation would suggest that the aim of reaching the '120,000 most troubled families' in the country, at least in the early stages of the TFP was compromised by the way in which the families were identified and by the choice of outcomes to be measured. Getting children back into school and reducing ASB are realistic goals for intensive outreach approaches and were amongst those most likely to be achieved by FRP workers. However, for some of the most troubled families, 'anti-social behaviour' was not identified as a cause for concern, and for others there was no child of school age or a teenager not in employment or education, so they would be 'missed off the list'. Parents gaining or preparing for employment was not a realistic aim for most of the parents in these families at the time of referral to FRP (though for some it became an aim towards the end of the service) so there would be a disincentive to include them in Payment by Results programmes that had this as a key outcome measure for funding purposes.

The major aims of improving the wellbeing of the children, or the health and wellbeing of parents so that they were more available to their children, did not figure in the TFP aims, and indeed were not ones that can be easily measured in order to trigger payment. A further reason why highly troubled families with the characteristics of those provided with a FRP service may be missing out on the not insubstantial funds that go with the TFP is the emphasis on this service being provided by non-social workers and kept separate from statutory child protection and children-in-need social work teams. This makes continuity of service for family members difficult to achieve, since a referral for a formal child protection or 'in need' assessment can lead to the interruption of service from an outreach worker the parents may be beginning to trust. For unitary authorities such as Westminster and Wandsworth this problem has been overcome by the integration of an FRP-style multidisciplinary service for the most troubled families within the overall TFP (White et al. 2014). However, in non-unitary authorities, although funding for the TFP is usually channelled through the children's services department, the outreach service is mainly provided at district council level or by the voluntary sector. This makes it more difficult to achieve two key elements of the FRP relationship-based service: ensuring, for as long as needed, continuity of a multidisciplinary 'team around the child and family'; and appropriate attention to the health and wellbeing needs of the parents whilst meeting the safeguarding and longer-term wellbeing needs of the children.

References

Brandon, M. and Thoburn, J. (2008) 'Safeguarding children in the UK: a longitudinal study of services to children suffering or likely to suffer significant harm.' *Child and Family Social Work 13*, 365–377.

Broadhurst, K., Wastell, D., White, S., Hall, C., Pechkover, S., Thompson, K., Pithouse, A. and Davey, D. (2009) 'Performing 'initial assessment'. Identifying the latent conditions for error at the front door of local authority children's services.' *British Journal of Social Work 40*, 2, 352–370.

Cabinet Office, Social Exclusion Task Force (2008) *Think Family: A Literature Review of Whole Family Approaches.* London: Cabinet Office, Social Exclusion Task Force.

Daniel, B., Taylor, J. and Scott, J. with Derbyshire, D. and Neilson, D. (2011) *Recognising and Helping the Neglected Child: Evidence-Based Practice for Assessment and Intervention.* London: Jessica Kingsley Publishers.

Department for Children, Schools and Families (2010) *Think Family Toolkit: Guidance Note 5.* London: Department for Children, Schools and Families.

Department of Health (1995) *Child Protection: Messages from Research.* London: HMSO.

Featherstone, B., White, S. and Morris, K. (2014) *Re-imagining Child Protection: Towards Humane Social Work Practice.* Bristol: Policy Press.

Kendall, S., Rodger, J. and Palmer, H. (2010) *Redesigning Provision for Families with Multiple Problems: An Assessment of the Early Impact of Different Local Approaches.* London: Department for Education.

Thoburn, J. (2010a) 'Acheiving safety, stability and belonging for children in out-of-home care. The search for "what works" across national boundaries.' *International Journal of Child and Family Welfare 12*, 1–2, 34–48.

Thoburn, J. (2010b) 'Towards knowledge-based practice in complex child protection cases: a research-based expert briefing.' *Journal of Children's Services 5*, 1, 9–24.

Thoburn, J. (2013) '"Troubled families", "troublesome families" and the trouble with payment-by-results.' *Families, Relationships and Societies 2*, 3, 471–475.

Thoburn, J., Cooper, N., Connolly, S. and Brandon, M. (2011) *Process and Outcome Study of the Westminster Family Recovery Protect.* Norwich: UEA Centre for Research on the Child and Family.

Thoburn, J., Cooper, N., Brandon, M. and Connolly, S. (2013) 'The place of "Think Family" approaches in child and family social work: messages from a process evaluation of an English pathfinder service.' *Children and Youth Services Review 35*, 2, 228–236.

White, S., Morris, K., Featherstone, B., Brandon, M. and Thoburn, J. (2014) 'Re-imagining Early Help: Looking Forward, Looking Back.' In M. Blyth (ed.) *Moving On From Munro: Improving Children's Services.* Bristol: Policy Press.

York Consulting (2011) *Turning Around the Lives of Families with Multiple Problems: An Evaluation of the Family and Young Carer Pathfinder Programmes.* London: Department for Education.

CHAPTER 5

Troubled or Troublesome?
Children Taken into Care and Custody

CAROL HAYDEN AND CRAIG JENKINS,
INSTITUTE OF CRIMINAL JUSTICE STUDIES,
UNIVERSITY OF PORTSMOUTH

Introduction

Conceptually, the terms 'troubled' and 'troublesome' are associated with different but overlapping problems and behaviours. Troubled behaviour is more suggestive of mental health problems and adversity. Troublesome behaviour is generally behaviour that affects others and connects more with concerns about anti-social behaviour (ASB) and criminal behaviour (Hayden 2007). So it is interesting to question why the decision was made to have a Troubled Families Programme (TFP). The national criteria for the TFP (crime/ASB, reducing worklessness and increasing school attendance) and the August 2011 riots as part of the initial impetus for the programme imply that troublesome (and costly) behaviour is the main focus of the programme.

Through the use of original research, this chapter explores the overlap between 'troubled' and 'troublesome' behaviour from the findings of a detailed study of 196 children who might initially be seen as either primarily troubled (children taken into care) or troublesome (children taken into custody). Some limited information on the wider family context of these children is included. The chapter starts with a consideration of terminology and behaviour in relation to the TFP and the wider policy context, briefly reviewing the evidence about the scale and nature of children and families with multiple problems. The chapter concludes with a short reflection on the TFP as a response to families with multiple problems and the role of social workers.

Troubled and troublesome behaviour

Terminology matters: very few practitioners working within local 'troubled families' programmes in England appear to refer to their service using the official terminology. This discomfort with the terminology affects how researchers and practitioners talk about the issues that are the subject of this chapter and how services present and name themselves to service users. Furthermore, the imposition of uncomfortable terminology complicates an already complex set of interconnecting issues and problems that feature in social work caseloads. On top of this, the focus and language of the work of child and family social work reflects attempts to capture family circumstances and needs within classificatory systems that illustrate both the ideology about the nature of the issues families face and the bureaucratisation of agency responses. That said, 'families with multiple problems' has gained some currency in recent years as a concept to describe families who have a range and depth of problems that are unlikely to be addressed by short-term social work interventions. Whether social workers are able to locate their work in this wider setting of inter-professional issues, as opposed to have their work 'collapse into a narrow residual niche concerned with the management of child abuse' (Spratt 2009, p.436) is an underlying concern of this chapter.

Changing behaviour is central to the work of the TFP, specifically the reduction of criminal behaviour and ASB, but this is also apparent in the promotion of 'responsible' and 'pro-social' behaviour – as in undertaking paid work and ensuring that children attend school. This focus on behaviour can also be seen in Family Intervention Projects (FIPs), which were established under New Labour before the TFP got underway. Some FIPs have been incorporated into TFPs. The origin of FIPs was in concerns about ASB and social housing. This emphasis on ASB in work with families is part of the refocusing of the work of social welfare professionals. As Parr (2009, p.1261) observes: 'traditional forms of social work interventions have become located within a discourse of tackling anti-social behaviour'.

There has been much debate about the judgements implied in the concept of some behaviour as 'anti-social' (Squires 2008). We have chosen instead in this chapter to refer to behaviour that causes concern as 'troubled' and/or 'troublesome' and to apply these concepts to evidence about the service involvement and behavioural needs of children taken into care and custody. The research is based on a cohort of 196 children taken into care or custody over a three-year period (2008–2011) in an urban unitary local authority. With the devolution of the responsibility for expenditure on custody to local authorities, this population tends to be grouped together as high-cost or 'tier 4' services in the UK. Prevention of entry into care and custody is often argued to be a good thing both socially and economically, with this co-joining of social and economic agendas in a 'future orientated investment strategy', which started under New Labour (Spratt 2009, p.345). The 2010 Coalition Government has continued this strategy. It follows that the use of research evidence to argue for a particular response to subpopulations identified as in need of intervention is now based on both social and economic arguments. The current research both serves and is critical of this agenda.

The research started as part of a needs analysis for a local authority that planned to set up an intensive service aimed at preventing entry into care and custody (residential schooling was added later). This intensive service became part of the local TFP. The focus of the service and our analysis is on an 'index child' within a family, so could be seen to fit with the whole family focus of the TFP. The overlap and interconnection between troubled and troublesome behaviour is evident in both the nature of our cohort (children who had been in care and/or custody) and the types of service involvement young people had over time. We identified key types of targeted and referred (tiers 2 and 3) service involvement as proxy indicators for early intervention with the children (prior to them being taken into care or custody). We were also able to get prevalence data on key aspects of adult behaviour.

The focus on the identification of particular triggers or indicators for early intervention with families who are likely to develop significant (if not necessarily complex) problems is relatively well researched (see for example Institute of Public Care (IPC) 2012). The kinds of carer or environmental factors that seem to contribute in particular to worse parenting and worse child outcomes are:

- parent mental health problems

- parent drug or alcohol misuse

- family offending or ASB

- domestic violence

- poor housing

- family debt (IPC 2012, p.11).

This list of factors overlaps with two of the indicators used to create the initial estimate for the TFP (mental health and poor housing) but not others (notably those to do with relative poverty and worklessness). Crucially, there are significant issues that are well known to interrelate with parenting and child outcomes (drug and alcohol misuse, domestic violence, offending and ASB) that are included in the list above but were not included in the data used to model the estimation of 120,000 families (2% of all families) for the initial phase of the TFP. To be designated 'troubled', families had to meet five of the seven criteria below.

- No parent in family is in work.

- Family lives in overcrowded housing.

- No parent has any qualifications.

- Mother has mental health problems.

- At least one parent has a longstanding, limiting illness, disability or infirmity.

- Family has low income (below 60% of median income).

- Family cannot afford a number of food and clothing items. (Levitas 2012, pp.4–5).

These criteria were taken from the Family and Children Survey (FACS) (Hoxhallari, Conolly and Lyon 2007). Levitas (2012, p.4) argues that a more apt description of the group identified by this survey is 'severely and multiply disadvantaged'. Crucially, as has been argued elsewhere (see Hayden and Jenkins 2013), this survey was primarily about parental vulnerability and relative poverty, not offending behaviour and school attendance. Nevertheless the TFP was launched with the expectation that local authorities would be able to identify a specified number of families in their area, according to the three national criteria of worklessness, crime and ASB, and children out of school. Significant for social workers is the complete lack of reference to children in need or child protection in the national criteria used to identify 'troubled' families.

Research on 'risk factors' in childhood and poor outcomes in adulthood is another way of profiling the constellation of issues and circumstances found in families with multiple problems. Some risk factors are additional to those listed above (IPC 2012; Levitas 2012), some are interrelated and some are the same. Risk factors include: low income, low attainment, poor social and emotional skills, poor parenting, low birth weight, poor parental mental health and living in a deprived neighbourhood (Spratt 2009). We also know a great deal about very specific service responses as an indicator that a child is presenting behaviour that is viewed by professionals as highly problematic. For example, we know that exclusion from school (particularly primary school and particularly permanent exclusion) is a good indicator of highly troubled and troublesome behaviour and that the effects of this rejection and the circumstances that go with it tend to act as a trigger for further adverse outcomes (Holt 2011; Parsons et al. 2001). If the excluded child is already known to social services, problems are more likely to continue and escalate as the child gets older compared with excluded children who have no involvement with social services (Parsons et al. 2001). More broadly, evidence suggests that it is the number of indicators present that is predictive of poor outcomes (Feinstein and Sabates 2006). Spratt (2012, p.1574) argues that 'multiples matter' in relation to 'cumulative adversity' and the likelihood of poor outcomes. Whether this is due to a multiplier effect (as illustrated by the work of Rutter 1979) or additive (Felitti *et al.* 1998), it is concluded that past a threshold of three or four risk factors outcomes worsen dramatically.

However, epidemiological studies have established that the experience of major problems or risks (often referred to as 'adversity') in childhood is more common than can be adequately dealt with by the child protection and criminal justice systems, leading to the conclusion that only a minority of children facing adversities such as child abuse, domestic violence, substance misuse and so on are identified by social services (Spratt 2012). It follows that estimates of how many families have multiple problems depends on where the line is drawn in terms of the number and type of adversities or risks used to create the estimate. Until recently there was no dedicated attempt to identify and track such families across agencies at a local level (Spratt and Devaney 2009). Indeed, Spratt (2009, p.440) argued that the 'systems to locate these families have not yet been developed'.

Nevertheless, the belief (in political circles at least) that it was possible to immediately identify families by the national criteria is illustrated in the speech by Prime Minister Cameron at the launch of the TFP (in December 2011) in which he said:

> We need to move quickly from broad estimates to actual names and addresses. By February we want local authorities to have identified who the troubled families are, where they live and what services they use. (Cameron 2011, p.9)

Whilst it is true that the systems to identify families did not exist at the start of the TFP, the data did exist in different local authority and other organisational databases. The problem the TFP has had in compiling and monitoring data on families relates mainly to data protection and ethical concerns about the consent of families, as well as some specific IT issues. Whilst 'data sharing protocols' and the provisions of the 1998 Crime and Disorder Act can overcome some of the data protection concerns, they do not address the ethical issues nor some of the more practical IT issues in terms of how data is held, downloaded and transferred. In particular, data sharing about 'worklessness' was essential to the programme, as one of the three national criteria and as part of the Payment by Results framework. Access to Department for Work and Pensions (DWP) data should have been agreed nationally at the start of the programme (and wasn't) leading to wasted effort replicated across the country and leaving local authorities with difficulties obtaining the necessary data in the first year of the programme. Furthermore, the potential for uncovering benefit fraud was an additional built-in tension in a programme that sets out to work with the whole family and has reducing worklessness as one of its national criteria.

Implicit in much of the discussion above is relative poverty, which tends to underpin the circumstances of many families likely to be seen as 'troubled' and/or 'troublesome'. The capacity of parents to offer positive parenting depends in part on the wider social and environmental circumstances in which they live. Rutter (in Hayden 2007, p.63) refers to this as the 'permitted circumstances of parenting'. These circumstances include: adequate income and housing, good mental and physical health and employment compatible with family life, as well as the availability of support services such as good-quality childcare. Negative parenting is associated with problematic behaviour from children, which may be internalising ('troubled') or externalising ('troublesome').

As a response to complex families with multiple problems, it is interesting to note that the TFP is a non-statutory intervention. Families are asked to sign up to the programme, rather than being told that they must accept the help. However, such families may be facing other types of more coercive response at the same time, such as a threat of eviction or prosecution because of persistent absence from school. So signing up to the programme is not totally voluntary nor is it totally coercive, despite some of the tough talking from politicians early on in the programme. The semi-voluntary nature of the programme is both an advantage of the TFP and an inherent tension. For example, child welfare concerns are likely to be present in many (probably most) of the households (see local criteria for the programme and research evidence in this article) and statutory services (such as social services) may have to become involved in some cases. Hence, in some ways the TFP is another way of delivering state services to complex families with multiple problems that may initially bypass social services and other types of statutory intervention. This may make the service more acceptable to some families.

The focus on the whole family, rather than individual people, in the TFP is often heralded as a relatively new way of delivering services in the UK, but it actually has a long history in relation to social work with children and families going back to the 1960s in the UK and US. Thoburn *et al.* (2013, pp. 228–229) note the increased focus in social work in the UK on child maltreatment after the 1989 Children Act, despite 'a bewildering array' of Government (and part Government) initiatives targeted at 'families with complex problems'.

Research evidence

The research evidence in this chapter is based on a city with a total population of over 200,000, of whom approximately 46,000 are aged 0–19. The population is predominantly White; Black and Minority Ethnic groups make up about 11 per cent of the whole population and 14 per cent of children and young people. There are about 86,000 households and 30,000 contain only one person. The city is in the top 100 most deprived local authorities in England and has pockets of severe deprivation. The city scores low (over 300 out of 354 districts, where 354 is the most deprived) on the composite index of child wellbeing developed by the DCLG. The number of children taken into care or custody is between 60–70 per year. At any one time, well over 200 children are in care and up to 20 are in custody (under 1% of all 0–19-year-olds). The DCLG estimated that the city would have over 500 troubled families (DCLG 2011).

The cohort of 196 children was created in cooperation with the local authority in order to undertake a series of searches across agencies to profile their needs and service involvement. In addition, participation in a monthly steering group and in-depth interviews with the key agencies involved in this field informed the interpretation and analysis of the data, as well as the analysis of the local discourse in different agencies about the broader troubled families agenda. In essence this was a highly reflexive and applied piece of research that engaged with policy and practice discourse as it was emerging (see Hayden and Jenkins 2013 for more details).

There are clearly a number of ethical and data protection issues in conducting research of this kind. The research underwent ethical reviews (university and NHS review) that advised on how the data on the 196 children was compiled and kept. All searches were undertaken by staff in local agencies within their own service only and compiled into a single Excel database by the data handler. The Excel database had the names and addresses removed, and the data was imported into SPSS for analysis by the university.

It quickly became apparent that identifying the families around these index children was complex and subject to change. Morris (2013, p.4) highlights how the voices of families in her research 'resisted definition by household'. This is an issue that is crucial to how a reliable estimate of the scale of need in a city is developed and how professionals can work with and help whole families (as opposed to focusing on the individuals within them).

The cohort of children taken into care or custody

The cohort included all children aged 6–17 years (without a disability) who were taken into care or custody over a three-year period (2008–2011). The cohort of 196 children was predominantly made up of children who had been taken into care (81.1%, 159 of 196). However, there was an overlap between the children taken into care and those taken into custody in the same timescale. Over a quarter (26.5%, 52 of 196) had been in custody, of whom 15 had also been taken into care within the three-year period. Thirty-seven children were taken into custody only during the three years, but seven of them had also been in care outside the three-year timeframe. For the purposes of later analysis, we organised the cohort into three groups (see Figure 5.1).

- children who had been in care only during 2008–2011 (144, 73.5%)

- children who had been in custody only during 2008–2011 (37, 18.9%)

- children who had been in both care and custody during 2008–2011 (15, 7.6%).

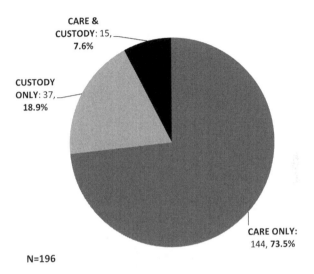

FIGURE 5.1 THE COHORT OF CHILDREN TAKEN
INTO CARE AND/OR CUSTODY (2008-2011)

Over half (115, 58.7%) the whole sample is male. This pattern changes when the sample is looked at in relation to care and custody. Slightly more than half the care only sample is female (84, 58.3%) and the great majority of those who have been in custody (84.7%, 44 of 52) is male (includes 'custody only' and 'care and custody').

The biggest ethnic group of children are 'White British'; these 151 children (77% of all children in the cohort) live in 119 households (75.8% of the 157 households). Therefore some of these households had more than one child taken into care or custody over the three-year period. 'White European' and 'White Other' groups together account for the next biggest ethnic groups (21, 10.7%), followed by Black (11, 5.6%) households (variously categorised as 'British', 'African', 'Caribbean' and 'Other'). There were three 'Gypsy/Roma' families, from which five children were taken into care. Ethnic groups not categorised as 'White' make up around one in eight (24, 12.2%) children and a similar proportion of households (22, 14.0%).

The 196 children lived in 157 households (which we refer to as 'families') with 231 adults (with some changes in household composition during the three-year period); 23 of these families had more than one child taken into care or custody. The 62 children (31.6% of the whole cohort) in these 25 families (15.9% of all families) differed from the families where only one child was taken into care or custody in some important respects. The 25 families can be characterised as having child welfare as the biggest issue in most cases. Less than a third (29%) had a record of offending behaviour, compared with nearly two-thirds (64.2%) of families with one child taken into care or custody. The children were significantly less likely to have a record of a violent offence or to come to the attention of crime prevention projects in the city. Where these children offended, they committed fewer offences. Only two children, from one of these families, spent time in custody. On average, the children were younger when they were first referred to social services, or when they had a Children and Young Person's Record (CYPR)[1] completed by the police (whichever came first). They were also younger when taken into care. In summary the city had a very small number of families (25 over a three-year period) that could be characterised as primarily vulnerable and in need of high levels of support for many (sometimes all) of their children.

A profile of need and service involvement

Figure 5.1 illustrates the profile of need and service involvement of the children. All data refers to a child 'ever' having been referred to or in receipt of a service. Offending behaviour and social services involvement are, of course, high because of the nature of the cohort. Figure 5.2 illustrates the searches on children undertaken within five main domains: educational problems, social work involvement,

---

1   CYPRs are completed by the police in relation to concerns about a child – these may relate to welfare and/or offending behaviour, for example, CYPRs are completed if a child is reported missing to the police. Research has demonstrated that very few children have multiple CYPRs completed on them (see Hayden 2007, pp.111–3).

referral to Child and Adolescent Mental Health Service (CAMHS), offending behaviour and record of concern from the police (CYPR). In essence these five domains cover a continuum of behaviours that might be seen as primarily 'troubled' or 'troublesome' and sometimes both.

An indication of some form of additional educational need (97%) and CYPRs from the police (96%) were almost universal across the group. Their high profile with the police is interesting given the age of the children: over a third (34.2%) of the children were under ten years of age in 2008 (15.8% in 2011). CYPRs are an indication of both troubled and troublesome behaviour and are sent by the police to children's social services to alert them of potential need and concern. Many of the children in our cohort were high profile in the city: the number of CYPRs for the group as a whole ranged from 1 to 74, with a mean across the sample of 15.5 records per child. Three-quarters (75%) had been referred to CAMHS and most were accepted. Nearly a third (32%) of the cohort spent some time in a special school in the city for children with social, emotional and behavioural difficulties. Over half (53%) had a record of offending and over a third (35%) had committed a violent offence. Nearly half (47%) had been referred to one of the city's crime prevention projects and over a quarter (28%) had spent time in custody. As noted above, the nature of the cohort explains why almost all had a record of referral to social services and most (166, 84.7%) had been looked after: either within the three-year period (159) or outside this period (7).

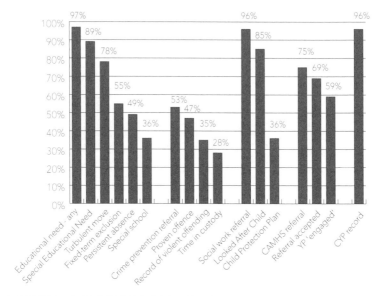

FIGURE 5.2 A PROFILE OF CHILDREN'S NEED
AND SERVICE INVOLVEMENT (N=196)

Housing tenure, adult issues and behaviour

We did not have access to reliable individual level data about where families lived, which can be seen as a proxy indicator of relative poverty. However, local authority prevalence data on the broader group included in the first year of the Troubled Families Programme in the city indicated that over two-thirds of the families lived in the more deprived areas of the city and that nine in ten families rented their homes either from the city council (over half) or privately (over a third).

Based on 231 adults recorded as co-resident with an index child at the point the child was taken into care or custody, a number of searches were undertaken within services as indicators of specific issues within the family. This data was provided as prevalence data across the sample so we did not have access to individual level information to check for accuracy. This should be kept in mind in relation to the prevalence data that follows. Nearly half (44.7%) of the adults were known to adult social care services. Over a quarter (27.3%) of adults were known to the probation service.

Around one in ten (10.4%) adults were known to have engaged with substance misuse services. In total, 8% of the adults had engaged or were engaging with the Domestic Violence Early Intervention Programme.

Table 5.1 is another way of profiling the differences across the cohort in relation to the number of indicators of need individual children had. To do this analysis we focused on 14 of the 17 indicators in Figure 5.1, removing 'educational need – any' because it is a composite of the other five educational indicators, and acceptance by CAMHS and engagement with CAMHS, as these indicators simply give more information on that type of referral. As all these indicators are for services or records of additional need outside the provision of universal services (or tiers 2 and 3 services – targeted or referred) they present some idea of the multiple adversities these children faced. Over a third (71, 36.2%) had ten or more indicators; over a half (110, 56.1%) had between five and nine; and the rest (15, 7.7%) had between two and four indicators. The overall mean for the cohort is 8.4 indicators.

Table 5.1 Number of indicators of need across the cohort (N=196)

Number of indicators of need*	Number in sample (N=196)	%
14	2	1
13	10	5.1
12	27	13.8
11	16	8.2
10	16	8.2
9	22	11.2
8	25	12.8
7	21	10.7
6	27	13.8
5	15	7.7

Number of indicators of need*	Number in sample (N=196)	%
4	9	4.6
3	5	2.6
2	1	0.5
1	0	0

*14 of 17 in indicators shown in Figure 5.1. Excludes the following three indicators: 'any' indication of educational need, 'acceptance' by CAMHS and 'engagement' with CAMHS.

Sequence of service involvement

Table 5.2 show the mean age of engagement with key targeted and referred services (and CYPRs) to provide some insight into the typical trajectory (or sequence) of agency involvement experienced by the whole cohort. On average (mean age across the cohort): children were referred to social services first, followed by being identified as having special educational needs (SEN), a turbulent school move, a CYPR being filed by the police, referral to CAMHS, being taken into care, school exclusion, attending a special school, referral to crime prevention intervention 1 (younger offenders), persistent absence from school, then a recorded first offence, crime prevention intervention 2 (older offenders) and, last, offending leading to custody.

The age range for referral to each service (youngest to oldest) is most marked in relation to referrals to social services and the child being taken into care, followed by referrals to CAMHS, then having a CYPR filed by the police. Thereafter, identification of SEN and attendance at a special school also has a very wide age range, as do other school based issues. The crime prevention projects were involved with nearly half (92, 46.9%) of all young people in the cohort and the majority (84, 80.8%) of young people with a record of offending.

Table 5.2 Age in years at which a child was...

First...	Number	Age		
		Mean	Youngest	Oldest
Referred to social services	188	8.77	0.08	17.25
Identified SENs	167	8.89	2.99	16.27
Turbulent move	147	9.93	4.51	16.38
CYPR filed by the police	188	10.40	1.75	16.58
Referred to CAMHS	144	10.74	1.16	17.33
Taken into care	166	11.10	0.08	17.75
Exclusion	104	11.50	7.09	16.19
Attended special school	63	12.30	2.24	16.38
Crime prevention intervention 1 (younger children)	59	12.38	6.50	16.91
Persistent absence	92	12.49	5.67	16.35
First recorded offence	104	13.28	10.08	16.75
Crime prevention intervention 2 (older young people)	70	14.82	12.16	17.91
Sentenced to custody	55	16.25	12.16	18.16

Troubled or troublesome? Comparing subgroups across the cohort

As we described earlier, the cohort in this study is made up of three main groups: children who were taken into care, children taken into custody and children taken into both care and custody during the three-year period (2008–2011). Table 5.3 explores the extent to which each of these subgroups has indications of both troubled and troublesome behaviour. It should be re-emphasised at this point that in each case we are referring to records that a particular referral or need was ever the case for a child. So the proportion with SENs refers to the proportion of children ever on the local authority SEN audit.

Table 5.3 Comparison of subgroups across the cohort

	Care only (N=144)	Custody only (N=37)	Care and custody (N=15)
Mean age (cohort start, 2008)	10.09	15.20	15.06
Gender	48% M; 52% F	80% M; 20% F	92% M; 8% F
Mean number of indicators overall	7.37	8.63	11.40
Special educational needs (SEN)	89.2%	87.5%	88%
Behavioural SEN	46.8%	62.5%	80%
Special school	26.6%	54.2%	72%
Experienced a turbulent move	77%	83.3%	80%
Mean number of turbulent moves	3.28	3.70	3.35

Persistent absence	46.8%	62.5%	48%
Excluded from school	42.4%	91.7%	92%
Mean number of exclusions*	7.64	10	9.65
Mean number of days lost to exclusion	15.92	27.14	26
Record of offending	34.8%	100%	100%
Mean offence severity**	2.81	3.32	3.24
Record of violent offending	19.9%	66.7%	80%
Mean number of offences	7.20	19.13	34.04
Referral to crime prevention project 1	23.3%	40%	68%
Referral to crime prevention project 2	23.4%	63.3%	72%
Social services referral	100%	73.3%	100%
Mean number of social services referrals	2.82	4.64	3.40
Ever had a Child Protection Plan	43.3%	16.7%	16.0%

	Care only (N=144)	Custody only (N=37)	Care and custody (N=15)
Referred to CAMHS	78.1%	55.2%	84%
Accepted by CAMHS	71.1%	50%	77.3%
Engaged with CAMHS	63.3%	34.6%	59.1%
Mean number of CAMHS referrals	2.69	2.19	3.29
CYPR	96.5%	90%	100%
Mean number of CYPRs	14.49	14.00	27.84

*Excluded from school: fixed period only, there were very few records of permanent exclusion across the cohort (seven in all).

** Mean offence severity as recorded by the Youth Offending Team: 1–8 with 8 being most severe. e.g. 1 = public/private transport fare evasion; 3 = theft and handling stolen goods; 8 = rape.

Overall, Table 5.3 compares the indicators of need and service involvement across the three subgroups within the overall cohort in this study (as shown in Figure 5.1). The 'care only' subgroup (N=144) is the biggest, it is also more evenly balanced between males and females and the mean age is much younger than the other two groups. The other two subgroups – 'custody only' (N=37) and 'care and custody' (N=15) – are predominantly male and older.

There are some interesting similarities and differences across these three groups: a similar proportion (nearly 90%) across all three groups have been assessed as having SENs during their schooling, but a higher proportion is for behavioural needs in the 'custody' and 'care and custody' subgroups in comparison with the 'care only' group. A higher proportion of children in the 'care only' group were assessed as having learning difficulties. A very similar proportion of children (around 80 per cent) across the three groups had experienced a 'turbulent move' of school three or more times. A 'turbulent move' refers to children moving school during the school year and/or within a school phase (primary or secondary). In effect this indicates the disruption to schooling often associated with care and custody placements. A CYPR was almost universal across the three groups.

There were more differences in the offending indicators across the three groups, although the proportion in the 'care only' group is interesting to note (34.8%) given the low mean age of this group at the start of the cohort. The pattern of referrals, acceptances and engagement with CAMHS is similar in the 'care only' and 'care and custody' groups, but the 'custody only' group shows lower levels of referral, acceptance and engagement with CAMHS.

In sum, all three groups have indicators of both troubled and troublesome behaviour but the emphasis varies. The biggest group – 'care only' (N=144) – is probably better characterised as more troubled than troublesome. Whilst over a third (34.8%) have a record of offending, they are much less likely to have a record of a violent offence than the other two groups and they are less likely to be excluded from school. The 'custody only' group (N=37) is generally both troubled and troublesome, but is probably seen as primarily troublesome. This group has a lower rate of referral to social services, CAMHS and crime prevention projects (in comparison with the 'care and custody' group). The mean number of CYPRs is similar to the much younger 'care only' group. However, exclusion from school data (suggesting troublesome behaviour) is similar to the 'care and custody' group. Interestingly, the 'custody only' group has a lower mean rate of recorded offences compared with the 'care and custody' group (19.13 compared with 34.04) but a similar mean severity score. Two-thirds (66.7%) had a record of committing a violent offence, compared with eight in ten (80%) of the care and custody group.

On most indicators, the 'care and custody' group (N=15) is the most troubled and troublesome: 80 per cent of this group have behavioural special educational needs (SEBD), most (72%) have attended a special school and have a record of fixed period exclusion (92%). Most (80%) have a record of violent offending, with a mean of over 34 recorded offences overall. This subgroup has the highest rate of referral and acceptance by CAMHS and the highest number of CYPRs (27.84). The number of CYPRs from the police illustrates the high profile and elevated levels of concern about this small group of young people.

Discussion and conclusions

The focus on children in this study with limited information about family circumstances provides some idea of the multiple adversities and subgroups within a cohort of children taken into care and custody by a city local authority over a three-year period. Although there is an average trajectory in terms of the route through specialist services and evidence of concern, the differences across the cohort are also worth noting. For some children, there was the long slow escalation of concern and service involvement; for others, the escalation to care (in particular) appeared to be rapid. For example, at one end of the continuum from primarily troubled or vulnerable to primarily troublesome is a case of a six-year-old child taken into care with low prior levels of service involvement, although she had first been referred to CAMHS at age three. Her primary school had clearly picked up that she had additional support needs. At the other end of the continuum is a very troubled and troublesome case that had very high levels of service involvement. Social services were already involved with the family when the individual was two years old. He went on to attend a crime prevention project when he was nearly seven and was first taken into care at age seven. His first recorded offence was at age ten. He had 51 records of offending by age 14 when he was taken into custody. Other differences in the balance between vulnerability and troubled and troublesome behaviour can be seen across this cohort (as in the three groups in Figure 5.1 and Table 5.3). The 25 families with multiple children who were taken into care are another grouping, with all but one family located within the 'care only' sample; as we have already noted, they are characterised primarily by their vulnerability in most cases.

Focusing on behavioural indications of need has its merits as a starting point for profiling the similarities and differences across a cohort such as this. It gives a sense of the extent to which children are presenting behaviour that concerns professionals in different settings (particularly in school and in the community). The data presented did not capture all the adversities these children and young people faced, such as relative poverty, the changing adults in their lives or parents who had mental health problems. These are families with multiple problems that may be reduced or ameliorated by the work of skilled professionals. Given the range of needs, multi-professional work is essential. Whether support workers working within the TFP can coordinate the help needed in a more effective way and reduce the use of care and custody remains to be seen. The latest figures at the time of writing do show a small drop in care applications in 2013/14, with Child and Family Court Advisory and Support Service (CAFCASS) suggesting that this could be due to earlier intervention to support families in crisis and Association of Directors of Children's Services (ADCS) arguing that the change illustrates better practice in terms of assessments (Lepper 2014). However, the political rhetoric about families 'turned around' does not begin to acknowledge whether this is meaningfully possible. The British Association of Social Workers (BASW) is critical of the TFP, saying:

> There is little evidence that this scheme is producing long-lasting change and yet millions of pounds of public money continues to be ploughed into it… It is ironic that the austerity agenda being pursued by the government is pushing families already facing difficulty to the brink and helping to create some of the social problems the initiative is trying to fix. (Hayes 2014, paragraphs 5 and 6)

It all depends on what we believe and know about the circumstances that help to create families with multiple problems. At the time of writing there is an increase in popular acknowledgement that unequal societies are unhealthy societies with increased levels of social problems than more egalitarian societies (McVeigh 2014; Monaghan 2014). The extent to which there is a political will to address this issue remains to be seen. Meanwhile, averting a crisis (such as entry into care and custody) is a laudable aim but underlying that objective are a host of other issues that may be associated with different individuals in a family that will need addressing if sustainable changes are the goal. The developing role of social workers in relation to the troubled families agenda will be interesting. Some, of course, are already working within TFPs in various types of 'support worker', 'key worker' or other role. Others remain focused in statutory roles within social services departments with limited time to become involved with the TFP. Whether the ambition of the TFP to transform the delivery of services to families with multiple problems is possible remains to be seen.

References

Cameron, D. (2005) *Troubled Families Speech.* London: Cabinet Office and Prime Minister's Office. Available at www.gov.uk/government/speeches/troubled-families-speech, accessed on 11 October 2014.

Cameron, D. (2011) *David Cameron's speech on plans to improve services for troubled families.* Available at www.gov.uk/government/speeches/troubled-families-speech accessed on January 26th, 2015. Cabinet Office: London.

Department for Communities and Local Government (2011) *Tackling Troubled Families.* Press notice, 15 December 2011. Available at www.communities.gov.uk/news/newsroom/2052313, accessed on 16 October 2014.

Feinstein, L. and Sabates, R. (2006) *Predicting Adult Life Outcomes from Earlier Signals: Identifying Those at Risk.* London: Centre for Research on the Wider Benefits of Learning, Institute of Education.

Felitti, V., Anda, R., Nordenberg, D., Williamson, D., Spitz, A., Edwards, V., Koss, M. and Marks, J. (1998) 'Relationship of adult health status to childhood abuse and household dysfunction to many of the leading causes of death in adults.' *American Journal of Preventative Medicine 14,* 245–258.

Hayden, C. (2007) *Children in Trouble.* Basingstoke: Palgrave Macmillan.

Hayden, C. and Jenkins, C. (2013) 'Children taken into care and custody and the "troubled families" agenda in England.' *Child and Family Social Work.* Available at http://onlinelibrary.wiley.com/doi/10.1111/cfs.12095/abstract, accessed on 11 October 2014.

Hayes, D. (2014) 'Social workers' leader criticises Troubled Families Programme.' *Children and Young People Now,* 7 May.

Holt, A. (2011) 'From Troublesome to Criminal: School Exclusion as the "Tipping Point" in Parents' Narratives of Youth Offending.' In C. Hayden and D. Martin (eds) *Crime, Anti-Social Behaviour and Schools.* Basingstoke: Palgrave Macmillan.

Hoxhallari, L., Conolly, A. and Lyon, L. (2007) *Families with Children in Britain: Findings from the 2005 Families and Children Study (FACS).* Research Report 424. London: DWP.

IPC (2012) *Early Intervention and Prevention with Children and Families: Getting the Most from Team Around the Family Systems*. Oxford: Oxford Brooks University. Available at http://ipc.brookes.ac.uk/publications/pdf/Early_Intervention_and_Prevention_with_Children_and_Families_June_2012.pdf, accessed on 16 October 2014.

Lepper, J. (2014) 'Most councils report fall in care applications.' *Children and Young People Now*, 13 May 2014.

Levitas, R. (2012) 'There may be "trouble" ahead: what we know about those 120,000 "troubled" families.' *Poverty and Social Exclusion in the UK*. Policy Response Series No. 3. ESCRC: Swindon

McVeigh, T. (2014) 'Inequality "costs Britain £39bn a year": Thinktank puts a figure on the annual cost of the gap between rich and poor and calls for politicians to act.' *The Observer*, 16 March 2014. Available at www.theguardian.com/society/2014/mar/16/inequality-costs-uk-billions, accessed on 16 October 2014.

Monaghan, A. (2014) 'Bank of England governor: capitalism doomed if ethics vanish.' *The Guardian*, 28 May 2014. Available at www.theguardian.com/business/2014/may/27/capitalism-critique-bank-of-england-carney, accessed on 16 October 2014.

Morris, K. (2013) 'Troubled families: vulnerable families' experiences of multiple service use.' *Child and Family Social Work 19*, 2, 198–206.

Parr, S. (2009) 'Family Intervention Projects: a site of social work practice.' *British Journal of Social Work 39*, 1256–1273.

Parsons, C., Hayden, C., Howlett, K. and Martin, T. (2001) *Research into the Secondary Education for Children Excluded from Primary School*. London: DfEE.

Rutter, M. (1979) 'Protective Factors in Children's Responses to Stress and Disadvantage.' In M.W. Kent and J.E. Rolf (eds) *Primary Prevention of Psychopathology, Volume 3: Social Competence in Children*. Hanover, NH: University of New England Press.

Spratt, T. (2009) 'Identifying families with multiple problems: possible responses from child and family social work to current policy developments.' *British Journal of Social Work 39*, 435–450.

Spratt, T. (2012) 'Why multiples matter: reconceptualising the population referred to child and family social workers.' *British Journal of Social Work 42*, 1574–1591.

Spratt, T. and Devaney, J. (2009) 'Identifying families with multiple problems: perspectives of practitioners and managers in three nations.' *British Journal of Social Work 39*, 418–434.

Squires, P. (ed.) (2008) *ASBO Nation: The Criminalisation of Nuisance*. Bristol: Policy Press.

Thoburn, J., Cooper, N., Brandon, M. and Connolly, S. (2013) 'The place of "think family" approaches in child and family social work: messages from a process evaluation of an English pathfinder service.' *Children and Youth Services Review 35*, 228–236.

CHAPTER 6

'Troubled Families'
A Team Around the Family

RAY JONES, ANNA MATCZAK, KEITH DAVIS
AND IAN BYFORD, KINGSTON UNIVERSITY AND
ST GEORGE'S, UNIVERSITY OF LONDON

Introduction

The Coalition Government's TFP has had a relatively long gestation and crosses political boundaries. Indeed, 50 years ago the range of difficulties facing some families, and how families themselves may be helped to respond to these difficulties, was at the core of the argument in England and Wales that a 'family social service' (Hall 1976, pp.16–17) should be established to replace the separate children's, welfare and mental health services within local Government. It was the Labour Government-initiated Seebohm Committee (1968) that spawned the 1970 Local Authority Social Services Act and led to the advent, under a Conservative Government, of social services departments as a family social service.

This was at a time when Sir Keith Joseph was Secretary of State for Health and Social Security. He sought to tackle what became called the 'cycle of deprivation' (see Rutter and Madge 1976), where social problems were seen to be transmitted across generations within families – families who in the 1950s and 1960s had been labelled as 'problem families' (Cooper 1983, p.54).

So when Mr Blair became leader of the Labour Party and coined the phrase 'tough on crime: tough on the causes of crime'

(Blair 1995), there was a sense of déjà vu from the 1960s and 1970s, although the focus was now turned very heavily on anti-social behaviour (ASB) and its causes and consequences (Gregg 2010). Mr Cameron later explicitly linked the causes of the summer 2011 riots in London and elsewhere with 'troubled families' and announced that he would 'put "rocket boosters" under efforts to turn around 120,000 troubled families in the wake of recent rioting' (BBC 2011).

And just as 'problem families' could be seen as families who had problems, as well as families who created problems, the same Janus-faced perspectives have been inherent in 'troubled families' being as much, if not more, about families who cause trouble as well as being troubled (DCLG 2012). Indeed the TFP is defined as being about families who are causing trouble and nuisance, although the estimate of 120,000 families in England to be targeted for the programme is based on measures of family deprivation and difficulty rather than of ASB (Levitas 2012). The rhetoric and reality of the TFP does not stretch, for example, to families in severe poverty and who may be in difficulty and distressed but who are not seen as a nuisance (Talbot 2012).

With a history of 50 years of identifying the 'problem' and 'troubled' families issue, and with initiatives ranging from a 'family social services' to an emphasis on punishing ASB, it might be wondered what more might be tried. Unusually, and despite arguments that this was 'a classic case of policy-based evidence' (Gregg 2010), an evaluation of the Dundee Families Project (Dillane et al. 2001) indicated a way forward. A targeted, intensive 'Team Around the Family' approach was seen to have avoided evictions, with financial savings from children not entering local authority care and reduced costs to the police and courts.

These findings provided, in part, the impetus for the then Labour Government to roll out a programme of Family Intervention Projects, which themselves have been seen to have reduced 'trouble' caused by families as well as assisting families with their 'troubles' (see, for example, Action for Children 2013; DfE 2011) and with a more recent study of Westminster Council's Family Recovery Project (Thoburn et al. 2012) generating similar findings. But the researchers have usually been modest and guarded about the claims for effectiveness and success, as the studies have been limited in sample selection, sample size and data sources and without comparative or control groups. The research might be seen as indicative rather than conclusive, but this has been 'good enough' to date for politicians and policy makers.

Finally, this and other research on TFP is of relevance to the discussion of psychosocial and relationship-based social work (see, for example, Murphy, Duggan and Joseph 2013), spanning the personal and psychological (Ruch *et al.* 2010) and the social, and harnessing resources, for families (Turner 2009). It is a psychosocial model of working that was evident within the programme that was researched.

The research

The research reported below adds to the body of knowledge about programmes being badged as a part of the English TFP. It has general lessons for social work as well as suggesting that a national programme largely described and motivated by a focus on families causing 'trouble' may have significant potential to help families who are 'in trouble', an argument also made by Parr (2009). This, indeed, as will be reported, was the experience of the families.

Through a limited process of competitive tendering, the local authority awarded a research contract to a local university to gather the views of families and other agencies of its TFP, known locally as the Family Recovery Project (FRP). There had already been a Family Intervention Programme (FIP) in the area, but the FRP was a scaling up of the FIP with an expanded, dedicated, multi-professional team, with one manager, of workers seconded to the FRP from agencies who were partners in the FRP and who through staff time and cash provided the resources for the team.

The partner agencies included the local council's housing and education welfare services, the police, Jobcentre Plus, and the NHS mental health and community health trusts. Workers in the team included education welfare officers, employment advisors, youth workers, police officers, health visitors, a clinical psychologist, a community mental health nurse, domestic violence workers, drug workers and generic project workers. The manager and deputy manager both had backgrounds as children and families social workers but there were no social workers seconded as practitioners to the team.

The research plan was to interview the first 20 families who agreed to engage with the FRP and who were also willing to be interviewed for the research. The families would decide who within the family would meet with a researcher. The number of families referred to the researchers increased to 25, as three families did not respond to the researchers when they sought to make contact with the families and two families did not follow through on the agreed arrangements to meet with them.

A semi-structured interview schedule was developed following discussions with the FRP team about issues they thought it would be significant to explore with the families about their perception of the FRP and also took into account previous reports on 'troubled families' programmes. The interviews were conducted face to face (with one exception), mainly in the family home and with agreement were digitally voice recorded and subsequently transcribed to aid content analysis. Interview questions were deliberately open ended to capture a range of responses, but with subsequent verbal prompts for some questions to ensure key information was collected from the interviewees (e.g. with what other services have you and your family had contact in the past year). Interviews lasted between 30 minutes and 2 hours.

The majority of the interviews (17 out of 20) were undertaken only with the mother. In two families interviews were undertaken with mother and father together and in one interview a teenage daughter sat through the interview and made some comments. All interviewees were told that what they said would only be used in writing a general report, which would not identify them and that nothing that was said would be directly referred back to anyone else unless it caused serious concern about the safety of anyone or about any serious criminal behaviour.

The research process and instruments, including the information sheets for potential interviewees, consent forms and the interview schedules, received ethical scrutiny and approval from the university's faculty research ethics committee and research governance approval, on behalf of all the agencies, from the local authority.

Using the transcripts of the 20 family interviews, the initial content analysis stage involved different combinations of two researchers identifying key themes in each interview and then clustering the themes in to overriding categories. The researchers then met together to consider the categories created and to agree the categorisation to be used for capturing the key content in all the interviews. All the interview transcripts were then read again by a researcher who had not originally read that transcript and content coded against the categorisation that had been created.

Twenty-four interviews, with a similar process for the interviews and data analysis as described above for the family interviews, were also undertaken with managers (13) and practitioners (11) from 12 agencies outside the FRP but who also worked with families and that through their work were likely to have some contact with or knowledge about the FRP. Some of the agencies were a part of the FRP's formal funding and management board partnership (such as the police, the health services and Jobcentre Plus). Others were not formally a part of the funding partnership but were working with the same families (e.g. local voluntary sector organisations).

In total, therefore, there were 44 interviews: 20 interviews with families and 24 with workers in other agencies.

The results

Characteristics of the families

These were not large families. Neither were they primarily young families. Figure 6.1 shows the number of children in the 20 families and Figure 6.2 shows the ages of the children. The families had a mean of 2.3 children with modal points of one child (seven families) and three children (six families). Only five families had four or more children. The mean age of the 46 children from the 20 families was 13.4 years with only three children (two families) under five years. The modal points were age 16 (five families) and 9, 10 and 19 years (four families each). There was a tail of older sons and daughters into their late teens and twenties still living in the family home.

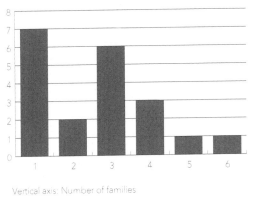

Vertical axis: Number of families

Horizontal axis: Number of children in family

FIGURE 6.1 NUMBER OF CHILDREN PER FAMILY

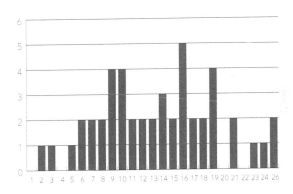

Vertical axis: Number of children

Horizontal axis: Age of children in years

FIGURE 6.2 AGES OF CHILDREN

For some families, the young adults had considerable influence within the family, disempowering the mother and imposing on the younger children. They often were peripatetic, coming and going, in bed in the mornings, around the house during the day and then out late at night, returning home late into the night and sometimes bringing friends home to sleep on the sofa. However, it was their behaviour outside as much as within the family home that had been a cause of concern, with many, but not all, of the young adults having been involved in ASB and criminal activities with contact with the police and courts.

A particular characteristic was that 16 of the 20 families had a single parent mother. There were no single parent fathers. Only four families had a mother where the father or a partner was also resident in the family home. Some of the mothers had non-resident boyfriends, and some families had continuing contact with non-resident fathers, but this was often a problem with the threat and danger of continuing harassment and violence.

Although this was not a specific issue explored in the interviews, most of the families had roots local to the area in which they lived and had other extended family members living nearby. They may still, however, have been isolated from their wider family who may themselves have been a worry and a hindrance because of their mental health or alcohol misuse.

Ethnicity and race was not explicitly explored within the interviews, and interviewees were not asked to identify their ethnicity, so it is not appropriate to comment in detail on this within this research report. But families involved in the study were known to include White British, Black British and Mixed Race relationships and children. There were no recent immigrants involved within the study and the research team were not aware that any of the families had ethnicities related to India, South East Asia or the European mainland.

Contact with other agencies

In addition to their involvement with the FRP, the families also had a wide range of contacts with other agencies. Of the 20 interviewees, 17 specifically mentioned when asked that they or other family members had had contact with a GP in the past year. As a part of a universal health service, and the front door to this service, this may not be unusual. However, it takes on a greater significance when 14 of those interviewed (who were very largely the mothers) said that one of the difficulties for them and their families was that they were depressed or very anxious and that this was the main reason for the GP contact, and for three mothers this was along with long-term physical health conditions and impairments. Six families were in contact with adult mental health services, in addition to contact with the GP, and three families with Child and Adolescent Mental Health Services (CAMHS). Only one family stated that they were in contact with a health visitor, probably reflecting that these were not primarily families with very young children, and one family said they had contact with a speech therapist. It was mainly GPs and mental health services, however, with whom the families, and mainly the mothers, had contact.

After GPs, the next most frequently mentioned other agency with whom the families had current or recent contact were children's social services and social workers (16 families) because of concerns about the care of children. Several families currently or previously had children in care, and several others had children with Child Protection Plans.

Not surprisingly, as the majority of the families had school-aged children, 14 of those interviewed (and these were all adults and primarily mothers) had had contact with one or more schools in the past year. This may not seem exceptional, but the nature of the contact was not primarily about parents' evenings and events but because of issues and problems, as illustrated by 13 families having contact with education welfare officers, with 12 families having issues about school non-attendance, and two each having had difficulties concerning a child's behaviour at school, school exclusion or parent's conflict with a school. Only three families mentioned contact with nursery or early years services, again reflecting that the families largely had older children.

Fourteen families had had contact with the police during the past year. This was also related to five families having contact with courts, four families having contact with a youth offending team, three families having contact with prisons and one family being in contact with the probation service. In a range of ways, therefore, the majority of families had some engagement with the criminal justice system, albeit primarily the police as a consequence of neighbourhood disturbance and complaints and conflict, abuse and violence within the home, and with families also sometimes the victims as well as perpetrators of disturbance locally.

A majority of the families (12) stated that they had contact with the benefits agency Jobcentre Plus, but this is probably an undercount of the number of families where at least some adults were in receipt of income benefits, as contact with Jobcentre Plus was usually only mentioned when there were issues and concerns about benefits.

Housing was also a significant issue for a majority of the families with 11 families having contact with the council's housing services in the past year with concerns about overcrowding (eight families), repairs and maintenance (seven families), damp (three families) and vermin and infestations in the house (three families).

There were a range of voluntary sector agencies with whom families were in contact. These included Well Care (three families), Family Action (three families), Citizens Advice Bureau (two families), Kids Company (two families), Catch 22 (two families), and a Young Carers Project (one family). In total there were 13 declared contacts with a range of voluntary agencies.

The families' views of their difficulties

So what was the range of difficulties that those who were interviewed saw within and for their families? Possibly surprisingly when the national policy profile is about trouble caused by families, the most frequently expressed family difficulty was the mother's, and in one family the father's, mental health. In 14 out of the 20 interviews, mothers spoke of their depression and anxiety states for which they were receiving treatment – primarily medication but two mothers also had or were receiving counselling. It would be difficult to unravel whether the mother's depression was a cause or consequence of other difficulties within the family, but its prevalence was significant.

Less surprisingly, for 12 families the behaviour of a child or children was generally seen as a difficulty, and this more specifically included children's ASB outside the home (seven families) and children's aggression within the home (five families). Through the interviews it also became apparent that for at least six families children were fearful for their mothers who were depressed (and in some instances had attempted suicide) or who abused alcohol. Seven of the families also had a history of domestic violence and in some instances children were afraid of leaving a mother who had experienced violence, especially when the perpetrator was still an active threat, and in four families where there was a partner or husband in the family home, conflict between the parents/partners was seen as a difficulty.

The children who were fearful for their mother contributed to the relatively high number of families (12) where school non-attendance was a concern and also to the five families where children's aggression in the home was seen as a problem with children fearful for their mother but also possibly resentful of how the mother's depression impinged on them.

The difficulties created by older sons and daughters were also noted within two families, as was the not necessarily unrelated trouble with neighbours (two families). Drug and alcohol misuse was also an issue (eight families), but this was as much about alcohol misuse by the mothers as much as by older sons and daughters.

The difficulties experienced by families were not only or primarily about their own behaviours. Problems also related to poverty, deprivation and housing. The welfare changes that came into force in April 2013 are very likely to have compounded and intensified these difficulties.

Ten families identified debt and financial problems as a difficulty, with five families specifically referring to the impact of unemployment, especially for older sons and daughters. Other family difficulties that were noted included the learning disability of a child (four families) and the mental health of a child (three families).

The overall picture is of families with a combination of difficulties that impinged on all family members including children, but with a high incidence of depression amongst single parent mothers. The mothers often seemed to be worn down and worn out and to be overwhelmed by a cluster of problems that created stress and worry, and not to be in control of what was happening to them personally or in the family home. The homes were overcrowded and, with very limited income, financial problems were significant. This was compounded by older sons and daughters being unemployed and still living in the family home making little financial contribution within the family.

The families' views of the FRP

Why families agreed to be involved with the FRP

Why did the families agree to be in contact with the FRP? For 13 families, they expected that the FRP would focus on helping the parents. Ten families expected help with children. Seven families hoped the FRP would help with issues with other agencies, such as 'sorting out housing' or avoiding care proceedings, eviction or ASB proceedings. More specifically, when asked why they had been referred to the FRP, 11 families said it was to deal with the behaviour of the children and two families said it was to deal with the behaviour of older sons and daughters. It was not only about children, as for six families it was said to be about the family in total and also for six families it was about assisting the parents, usually a mother.

There was also a recognition that families were referred to the FRP to delay and possibly prevent other actions being taken. This included stopping children being taken into care because of child protection concerns (eight families), avoiding prosecutions of parents for children's non-school attendance (six families) and avoiding eviction (four families).

Other reasons noted by families as to why they had been referred to the FRP included to tackle parents' alcohol misuse (two families), because the mother had taken a drug overdose (one family), to work on getting a child returned from care (one family) and because the parent had stopped engaging with the social worker from children's services (one family).

The families' experiences of the FRP

What did the families experience from their engagement with the FRP? This was the focus of much of the interviews and it generated a wide and rich range of responses, which are listed below.

- intensity (eight families)
- frequency (ten families)
- reliability (three families)
- flexibility (four families)
- accessibility (seven families)
- responsiveness (eight families)
- confidence building/motivation (seven families)
- challenging/confronting (four families)
- boundary setting (three families)
- establishing routine/structure (seven families)
- demanding/strict (four families)
- understanding (five families)
- not conned (four families)
- relationships (five families)
- good listener/can talk to (nine families)
- help to deal with complexity of lots of issues (six families)
- mediation with other family members (two families)
- negotiate/mediate with other agencies (thirteen families)
- range of workers/multiagency (eight families)
- works with all/several different family members (eight families)
- works on different issues (five families)
- takes action/does things (ten families)
- provide practical help (six families).

These are not the responses to a checklist; instead this is a categorisation of responses freely given by those interviewed about what they experienced the FRP did and was like. Clusters of themes emerged from these family responses.

First, there were responses about the intensity and frequency of the work of the FRP and the amount of face-to-face and telephone contact with families:

> So they allocated a key worker because the key worker does [walk with mother to address her anxiety about going out]. And I also got involved with the drug worker because I was getting cravings again because I used to take drugs three years ago…and they were both taking it in turn to walk me and to have one-to-one meetings Monday to Friday, 9 o'clock every morning, from 9 until I pick up [pre-school daughter] which was like 1 o'clock and then they'd leave me.

Second, the FRP was seen as accessible and flexible, and this included being willing to change workers in contact with a family if this was not working well for the family and also changing the focus of the FRP's activities if needs changed over time:

> And they tend to work around me as well, where the other people…Because I start work at 8 o'clock in the morning and I sometimes come home at 11/11.30 and then I go back at 1.45 because I get a break in between, so if there's any meetings like that, or they come down, they try to do it in that time.

But the FRP was also seen as challenging, demanding and strict, setting explicit plans and expectations and pursuing the plans with energy and rigour and with workers not easily conned or fooled:

> Yeah, it's good because I do need that kick up the bum, and a bit more hands on, and that's why they are good for me.

And:

> They are like 'Well what do you want? This is what we offer.' So it's clear guidelines as well and it's assertive.

One of the particular attributes of the FRP was helping parents to get back some control and order in their lives. This was especially important when there were multiple difficulties facing parents that were overwhelming. Creating some sense of order and regaining control from chaos was a special attribute identified for the FRP and was confidence building and motivating:

> She's helped me with my paperwork and she's a bit like a… not a pushy mum, but she really sort of like gets me going. She used to come in and like "Come on, we'll do this, we'll clean this up, and we'll do it today and have a bit of hoovering, a bit of mopping" and it's a bit more fun to tell you the truth.

Setting boundaries for children and creating a structure and routine was also seen as a particular focus of the FRP and its work with parents on parenting:

> In my opinion I think I was doing okay with my parenting skills but they obviously felt that I wasn't, and just to be…I am a bit of a softie. I think that was probably my downfall, that I was not being strict enough yeah, so yeah, just putting…That was an area that they were putting boundaries in, so I think I am starting to put boundaries in.

And this was achieved by having FRP workers who whilst being assertive and demanding, were also seen as building strong relationships:

> She is very understanding and I have got other personal problems that I can talk to her…I can really talk to her, she is really nice, we'd meet once a week in a coffee shop or something and we had someone to offload on but she'd also be very professional.

And:

> They are a lot more approachable, they are a lot more – you don't feel intimidated by them – well the ones I personally work with anyway.

The FRP workers also shared in tasks such as decorating, cleaning or cooking with parents or participating with children in leisure and sporting activities. This was experienced as potentially helping parents and children to move forward where previously they lacked confidence or motivation, even if sometimes the help offered was not taken up:

> They offered [son] to do workshops with like a gym, someone to take him to the gym but he never took it up, but I mean I thought it would have been a good idea.

Practical help possibly had a particular significance for those who had little positivity coming into their lives and were socially isolated and where life was always a struggle:

> ...she just comes and sees me and like I said I ain't seen her since before Christmas, but they gave me a hamper of food and I have never had anything like that and it's, you know, [GETS UPSET].

And:

> We'll talk and find out how [her son] is – sometimes, like I say, we did some cooking once. She gets him...oh, she's got him to go along to this place and got a bike which is brilliant.

It was this working with all or several members of the family on a range of issues that was seen as especially different from other agencies that tended to focus on only one issue of particular concern or within the brief of the agency and often did not engage most family members:

> They cover a load of things and where they have one person working with you and then they can go to each individual case of housing, social security and such like, and mental health teams, you know. I mean I have seen a counsellor guy from there, and I have struggled to see somebody.

Having a skills mix within the team, and being multiagency, were also seen as important:

Each one of them has a different role to play kind of thing, it's not like you're dealing with one person who deals with every problem that you have.

But the FRP was not only valued because it worked with and did things within families. The most frequent response of all (13 out of 20 families) was that the FRP negotiated or mediated for the family with other agencies:

They have helped with the three kids, like [FRP worker] has gone to the police station with us with [son], and social services wouldn't do that.

And:

...getting housing to do all the repairs that they were meant to have done months ago.

Help with other agencies was especially valued by parents – the single parent mothers – who often were having to juggle the demands of engaging with four, five or six different agencies, all of which worked separately and were unaware of the total aggregate of demands (e.g. to be available for home visits or to go to agency offices) from all the agencies. There was also the Kafkaesque experience of parents not being able to get a response from other agencies. Finally, the parents – and sometimes the children – may have been in dispute with an agency or under threat of what was experienced as punitive action from an agency and the FRP mediated and mitigated the continuing conflict or threat.

Did the families think the FRP was making a difference?
The responses below record the families' view about how they thought the FRP was making a difference.

- helping the parent(s) (fourteen families)

- more motivation (six families)

- providing structure (twelve families)

- providing parent modelling (one family)

- parents more confident/stronger (nine families)
- parents feel emotionally supported and backed up (five families)
- mental health of parent improved (three families)
- parenting behaviour changed/more boundary setting (thirteen families)
- parents now more reflective about parenting (four families)
- increased awareness of parents' impact on children (five families)
- child's behaviour has improved (six families)
- helping whole family/making family stronger (four families)
- getting older sons/daughters to change behaviour (two families)
- practical improvements (seven families)
- getting better with other agencies (four families).

What did these freely given responses from parents mean? First, the positive impact on the parents and parenting was noted for many families, with several parents stopping taking antidepressants:

> It's brilliant. It's amazing because they have made me face up to what I needed to deal with to be a better person.

And:

> My whole body was constantly aching and I didn't feel right all the time and so I was taking antidepressants back then, but since FRP have been helping me I am now off of them.

In particular, parents themselves felt supported and more motivated and had themselves changed and become more confident:

> I will miss them, but I'll be happy because it has given me my confidence back.

And:

It's the consistency and I feel like I have got someone backing me up.

Second, possibly as a result of changes for the parents or because of the direct work with children, for some families (albeit at the time a minority) positive change was seen in the children's behaviour:

> Yeah, I have more patience. I have more patience with her, and I didn't understand the point of the naughty corner, but it's as scary as shouting to be honest I found out because she doesn't like the naughty corner [daughter aged three]. Her behaviour has changed, she is more calm and listens to me a bit more. I think that's because I am calm within myself. Yeah.

But overwhelmingly the parents who were interviewed saw the impact of the FRP as largely on themselves and their parenting whilst some commented there was a positive impact on children or on the wider or total family.

Last, some parents were recognising that there had been practical improvements with, for example, rooms redecorated, broken furniture replaced or a boy provided with a bike, and some parents also noted that there had been an improvement in their relationships with other agencies or the other agencies had been more responsive.

There were, however, anxieties about what would happen when the FRP ended or withdrew:

> There is a change, there's been a shift, you know, up a bit, but it's not strong enough yet I don't think for them to back out yet.

There were also criticisms of the FRP, albeit much smaller in number than the positive comments. Criticisms included that there was nothing happening for a family or parents that they could not achieve on their own (three families) and that they had had no real choice about involvement with the FRP because of child protection concerns (two families):

> I had a reluctance because I've had professionals in my life for so long and I thought okay, it's probably going down the road again of having more professionals in, on top of the ones I have

already got, but I sort of...I had no choice really than to go down this road again...my hands are sort of tied, so I had to do it or else.

What was not welcomed by a minority of families was the intensity (three families) and intrusiveness (four families) of the FRP and that FRP workers were impatient (one family) or had judgemental attitudes (three families) and that review meetings were intimidating (one family):

> The only thing I did find with the FRP is that you feel very like claustrophobic because it's very intense, like no one tells you that when you sign up to it – they will come like three or four times a week to visit you. So I did find at some points with social services visits and the FRP, I was feeling a bit like intense, like claustrophobic, I had no free time to do anything at all, and I did say to them 'I am feeling a bit...it's a bit too much. No one said *how* direct you do work with us,' and they did back-off a bit.

And:

> I am a bit funny, I don't like being told what to do. I mean I am 51 years old, it's very difficult for me to be spoken to like.

There were also comments that some workers were young with no experience of being parents (one family), were not understanding (two families), were not easy to relate to (two families), were unreliable (one family), did not give good advice about benefit issues (one family) and were not open and honest (two families).

There were also comments that the FRP workers failed in seeking to get other agencies to help a family (three families), which mainly related to tackling housing issues, or did not give the practical help a family thought they needed, and there was also a view that a referral to CAMHS was what was really needed to tackle a child's behaviour. Three of the parents who were interviewed also expressed concern that they still had to see workers from other agencies. This was primarily about having still to see children's services social workers because of child protection concerns. One parent also said she thought the FRP was 'setting her up to fail'.

The families' views of the FRP compared with other agencies

What did the families think about the FRP compared with other agencies with whom they had contact? Four parents saw other agencies as less understanding and not listening, five saw other agencies as more threatening and four saw other agencies as less active.

Without exception, the 'other agency' chosen by the parents for their comparison with the FRP was children's services (social services) social workers with whom they had contact because of Child Protection Plans and possible care proceedings. These social workers were seen less regularly than the FRP workers, but often still weekly, and were primarily felt to be watching and monitoring what was happening to the children but without acting to change anything for the children, parents or family:

> Social services are there to help you and you're asking for help, you're telling them what you need and they don't really want to know. I mean some of the social workers come here, they are here five minutes and they have gone.

And:

> I have not really been involved with social services. I have had a social worker with the family when I was first ill, but with social services it's something you don't have a choice with – they come into your home and I don't particularly like social services, you feel like they are prying into your business.

The views of other agencies and workers

What did the practitioners and managers working in other agencies see as the strengths and weaknesses of the FRP? There was prevalent view that it was the multi-professional (16 interviewees out of 24) and multi-agency (14 interviewees) nature of the FRP that was a strength and that this allowed a 'holistic' service and created a team around the family (12 interviewees):

> Because it's a multidisciplinary team they aim to work with families who have got multiple complex needs, so they can access all those different services around them.'

And:

> It's around really getting to know people and being able to just bounce ideas of somebody from a different discipline who can give you some different ideas. I think that really helps, particularly when you are working with some really complex families.

The Team around the Family (TAF) was seen as a strength because the FRP then worked on a range of family issues (eight interviewees) and was able to mobilise a wide range of assistance for the family (11 interviewees). It also assisted the collation of information from across agencies (four interviewees). Secondments into the FRP from a range of agencies was seen to promote knowledge within the FRP about those agencies (two interviewees) and easier links with the agencies (three interviewees), and influencing other agencies on behalf of a family (two interviewees) was seen as being facilitated by the multiagency and secondment worker model of the FRP:

> Obviously the aspiration is that by targeting and working on these individuals, not as separate agencies but very much as one unit, well hopefully we'll stand a chance of actually tackling the core problems of those small core of troubled families, troubled families who give us the most difficulty.

And:

> I like the fact that it's a multidisciplinary team as well, that they have immediately got all those people around them which can support…where we have to do the referrals on to these other services, they have immediately got them there working, able to work with the family and support the family and it can all be done under one roof. The family is not having to deal with

five or six different agencies which can be overwhelming for a family sometimes.

The nature of the FRP's work was seen to be intensive (12 interviewees) and with time and space to work with families and build relationships (eight interviewees) and to provide extra support and assistance to families than was able to be provided by other agencies (eight interviewees). Interviewees from other agencies felt that families viewed the FRP as supportive (four interviewees) with work undertaken that was flexible (seven interviewees), as the FRP responded to the families' variable and varying needs that might change over time and with the FRP being able to assess a family through knowing a family well (three interviewees):

> For me the strengths [of the FRP] are that they can go into the family for several hours a day, several times a week I think is amazing…I think families which are really stuck, they really need that level of support and I think that's…there's not many services, if any really, which can offer that and I think it's brilliant.

The FRP was also seen, as also noted above by families themselves, as being responsive and adaptable if a family or family member was not finding it easy to engage with a particular FRP worker:

> I can speak [with the FRP] about maybe changing the way that they work with this particular family because they find it a little bit intimidating…because at the end of the day if you're not happy with the situation and things don't seem to be improving, then what's the point? We might as well try a different course.

Particular mention was made of the focus on parenting (six interviewees), parents' motivation and parents' mental health and its impact (five interviewees):

> The mum looked physically different, she was holding herself much better and she wanted to action some things herself and

when it was suggested she could have help with one particular area she said 'No, I want to do it myself.'

And:

I think the FRP bring in to quite a chaotic lifestyle a little bit more calm, a little bit more routine to a mother who was always struggling with her parenting skills.

It was noted that the FRP often worked with the most difficult families (11 interviewees) and with families where the work by other agencies had become 'stuck' (seven interviewees):

It's targeted at those people because they are seen as being the most difficult in terms of intervention and the most costly in terms of resources put into them right across the partnership.

And:

It's definitely targeting the hardest-to-help ones, the hardest-to-help means the harder problems, with multi-problems I would say.

If the families were not willing or able to engage with the FRP, this in itself was seen as significant in informing the assessment of the family, with the FRP as a 'last resort' for families (six interviewees) before more dramatic, and what they might see as punitive, action was taken:

...if they don't engage or don't continue to engage then the enforcement element becomes all the more stronger...you get a real insight into actually how their lives are running, and that may in itself raise issues around the welfare of children.

And:

[Clarity] is pretty good and I think that goes towards the first initial meeting where you lay everything out on the table, show them exactly what the repercussions and any further actions will be. I mean at that stage it's the last door saloon so to speak.

Finally, the FRP team was seen as energetic, passionate, committed and enthused (five interviewees) and being clear about their role and task (three interviewees):

> I found that they're really positive and passionate.

And:

> But I think a lot of that [success] stemmed from how [the FRP worker] delivered it. His enthusiasm is almost infectious. I think, 'Yeah, actually this is something'. So yeah, for him I can't...I mean he is dealing with one of my cases and then his colleague is dealing with the other one so...But they both have that enthusiasm, that drive, that yeah...to help resolve, to help, [but also] realistic at the end of the day, which is all important.

The FRP's weaknesses as seen by other agencies

What about any weaknesses in the FRP? Weaknesses were identified and mentioned much less frequently (32 interviewees) than strengths (165 interviewees), a ratio of 1:5, indicating an overwhelmingly positive perception of the FRP by the practitioners and managers from other agencies.

The most frequently mentioned weaknesses were the time-limited nature of the FRP's work with any family and a question of what will happen for families when the FRP involvement finishes (seven interviewees):

> I know they have the idea of stepping down to a service, but actually if they are offering so much intense support I don't know if they are offering a follow-up and it would be something which would be quite important, especially if they have worked really intensively with somebody for a whole year, to kind of stay there for six months or something. And even stepping down can be a bit scary, you know, the family must have built up a massive relationship with these workers and there must be a real trust and suddenly to have to work with another agency, it must be quite a...

There was also a concern that compared with the number of families that might benefit from engagement with the FRP, the numbers of families receiving the FRP services were small (six interviewees), thresholds were high and that being a part of early intervention would be helpful:

> It seemed very specific about why they were looking at families, you know, anti-social behaviour, maybe problems with housing, long-term involvement, subject to a CP [Child Protection] plan, so I have other families that don't meet the criteria that I think would benefit from quite intensive support but I wouldn't be able to refer them.

And:

> I think it's an excellent model. It's obviously very resource intensive, so that's the problem with those kinds of pieces of work, but if we could provide that for lots more families we all know, we'd make a real difference.

Other weaknesses mentioned infrequently were that the most troublesome families may not give consent to be referred to the FRP (three interviewees) and that getting family consent can be time consuming (three interviewees). This may also be reflected in the view that there might be a difference between compliance and commitment by families (two interviewees):

> It's difficult because it's voluntary and people at the beginning say 'Oh yes, that all sounds really good', but actually that's where the tension lies, getting people to…the question is, well when they step away, does it go back to what it was? One of the workers, who I quote, and I have told him I quote him, is you know, 'there's compliance but not commitment'

Other potential weaknesses each mentioned by one interviewee included: the FRP 'just delaying the inevitable' of, for example, eviction; the time it takes to complete the referral process; that the FRP's intensive and extensive involvement with a family can initially heighten concerns about the family as more information is gathered about their difficulties; that 'the FRP can come across to families as intimidating and a little too pushy'; and that there could be a temptation for the FRP to become 'little bit precious':

> There's a temptation to get a little bit precious about, you know, 'better than anybody else' even though some of the network, they have known the families for a lot longer and we all sometimes get into that...'Yeah, I'm the one seeing them every day, so I know, yeah'...I'm not saying that they're doing that but there is a little temptation to think they know best.

This comment about possible preciousness was explicitly countered by the comment that:

> I have not heard anybody (unless they say it when I am out of the office) but nobody has spoken negatively about the FRP and I think partly as well it's because of the way in which it's done. There's no arrogance from the FRP about what they do or the successes that they have, it's all been seen as partnership. We are all a part of the puzzle to help this family move forward.

One comment was also made that the FRP may be seen as a 'bit touchy feely' but that this was not necessarily a negative approach:

> I do a lot of anti-social behaviour [work] and I suppose some professionals may feel that the [FRP] can be a little bit touchy feely I think, without being dismissive of the whole process. But I think it's designed to be touchy feely in the sense you're going to need to work with these people, they're not there to tell them what to do so to speak, they are there basically to guide them.

Overwhelmingly, however, the comments from practitioners and managers in other agencies were positive, and this was also the weighting of the comments about how the FRP related to their agencies and the impact of the FRP on their agencies.

The FRP's relationship with other agencies

Five of the other agency interviewees noted that the FRP was proactive in communicating with them and their agency, and four gave comments more generally that the FRP was inclusive in its work with other agencies keeping them informed and involved:

> One of the things I liked about them was that they were going maybe possibly take the lead, but keep you updated on all the meetings. Every time they do a visit they send me a log. And they have asked me my advice on a lot of issues, so good communication.

And:

> We get weekly updates and telephone discussions. We do joint visits. It's very easy to engage with them.

Two workers from other agencies commented that communication was particularly good from the FRP to the worker and agency who had referred the family to the FRP but one stated it was less good if they were not the referrer but were still working with the family: 'you don't get any feedback [from the FRP]'.

Invitations from the FRP to attend meetings about particular families were seen to be good at keeping workers in other agencies involved and informed, but there were also two comments that these meetings were a time-consuming and extra-work demand for workers in other agencies.

Comments were made by three of the interviewees from other agencies that their agencies still held the statutory powers and responsibilities to take the 'tough decisions' about families:

> They don't, they cannot…they're not statutory, they're not able to do child protection visits…I wonder why it's a separate agency [to children's social services], I wonder what the thinking was around why it wasn't brought into children's specialist services, all the different parts of that, so that [children's social services] could have that, resources and funding.

And:

> But if they don't engage with the FRP or they don't improve, then obviously the ultimate sanction would still have to apply and again, with my manager's hat on I have to have due regard to

see how that progress is happening with FRP, to decide whether I am going to suspend any further legal action pending their engagement, or if their engagement isn't working i.e. they're engaging but their behaviour is not changing then enforcement action must continue.

But the FRP not having statutory powers, with these still held by the referring agencies, was not necessarily a weakness, as this comment indicates:

> I think there is something about it being separate, and I guess I say that having worked in the voluntary sector and seeing the benefits of being able to work with families when they know we aren't a part of children's services even if the referral came from there. I think if the FRP was part of children's specialist services it would perhaps feel like something else being done to families and I am not in favour of 'doing to families' – I am in favour of 'working with' and I think FRP does that. It gives a clear message to families that they are working with them – I think clearer than we are able to do because there's always a bit of stigma over children's specialist services no matter how we approach it. I think that's key to their success.

There were also two comments that the FRP shared the responsibility for decision-making and for the family with other agencies, and that the FRP reduced the workload of other agencies by taking on a responsibility itself and working with the family:

> All of a sudden it's not only the social worker trying to support the family.

And:

> They have saved me sleepless nights for which I am always grateful. Yeah, I think they…I mean time is money so they have saved us most definitely time, they have saved us time in terms of being able to bring the child protection process to an end, that we will be in a position to step out shortly. If you look at time as money in that respect, and for the amount of time and effort, if I think about these two families that the worker was

actually putting in, yeah, I would say they definitely saved us money in that respect.

Other comments, each only made once, were: that the FRP promoted multiagency understanding (one interviewee); that the FRP takes on board ideas and understanding from other agencies (one interviewee); that the FRP helps other agencies to see the wider needs for families (one interviewee); and the role of the seconded worker into the FRP was seen as positive in sharing information back with the agency:

> The adviser who is based in the FRP is getting a lot of knowledge from other agencies as well, so she is able to pick up some of the things which if she wasn't there, she might not know, which she then shares it with staff within [our agency].

There were a small number of one-off comments about the experiences of seconded workers into the FRP from other agencies. A positive comment was that the seconded worker was enlarging her competence through her membership of the FRP. Negative comments were that: '[the seconded] worker may not have been best used initially,' and that: 'the seconded worker had felt micromanaged in the team'. Building a multiagency and multi-professional team is not a quick, instant-fix task, but the overwhelming view as noted above was that it was the multi-professional and multiagency nature of the FRP that was one of its widely recognised strengths.

Comments from other agencies about improving the FRP

Were there any views from practitioners and managers in other agencies about how the FRP might be improved? There were very few suggestions for improvement but the few that were made clustered around expanding the FRP, making it available for more families and making it a part of earlier intervention (eight interviewees).

Three interviewees commented that the FRP should provide more information about its work to other agencies and workers:

We had a lot of information about the FRP at the beginning when it first came to [location] and we haven't had much information since then, so maybe updates of where they are with us, or their availability or…that would be something that would, you know…

And:

Another negative is that I don't think they are very well known.

Two interviewees suggested that the team might be strengthened by being more child centred, with the addition of a play worker (one interviewee) or a seconded children's social services social worker (one interviewee).

Did the other agencies see the FRP as value for money?

Was the FRP seen as being likely to be successful and good value for money? The most frequent comments were that the FRP would save public expenditure in the long term (seven interviewees):

It's working in a very intensive way with a small number of families on whom we seek to get the best return in actually changing some of their behaviour and therefore reducing demands on public services.

And:

I think there's very good reason to believe it could be [value for money]. It should be, yes, because I think if you look at the longer term…but the trouble is you don't know that until you have got the longer term outcomes, because actually the saving is not immediate for that kind of work. The saving is the hope that you have actually prevented some of these young people from getting into further offending trouble, from families from being evicted and having to be placed in hugely expensive B&B accommodation somewhere else in the country and losing all links with their networks and all the things that are going to happen to some of these families if we don't put the piece of work in.

Other positive comments were that the FRP improved the wellbeing of family members (six interviewees), that positive changes within families had already been observed (five interviewees), and that the FRP was reducing neighbourhood nuisance and fear (three interviewees) and helping the family to be a part of the community again (one interviewee):

> This [mother's improved mental health and motivation] has had a knock-on [effect] on her son whose attendance has really picked up. He has ups and downs about how he feels about school but she does not accept any nonsense, he comes to school and he is fine when he gets here, so he is still trying to play mum up but she is very strong and it's good, it's really very good.

And:

> Yeah, I think [the family] benefit in lots and lots of different ways and if they can get that family to be part of the community again, I reckon that has to be a benefit, not just for the family but for the locals, for us, for everybody involved in dealing with that housing, so yeah, I think they are good value for money.

There were also the comments noted above, however, about whether change within and for families will be sustained, and there was also a concern that lots of new initiatives have started in the past but then are brought to an end and could this also be the FRP's fate:

> Not to sound too pessimistic, but there've been so many initiatives which have been around to support families...

There were also one-off responses that: included families were engaging with health services (one interviewee) and immunisations increased for children (one interviewee); the FRP was improving understanding of families by other agencies (one interviewee); the FRP was getting family members into work (one interviewee); and the FRP was saving the time of other agencies (one interviewee) and overall was 'money well spent' (one interviewee).

Possibly not unrealistically, there were two comments that 'benefits will only be seen over many years' and that 'we need to wait and see as this is a new service'.

Concluding comments

First, some comments about the families who were interviewed. All the 20 families who were interviewed gave coherent and well-considered opinions about the FRP and its impact on them as a family. Altogether 25 families were referred to the research team for interviews, but the research team was unsuccessful in getting a response from five families.

The families were predominantly single parent families headed by a mother. The mother herself was often overwhelmed by the range of difficulties facing the family, with concerns about overcrowding and other housing issues and debt. There had often been a history of domestic violence and this was a continued threat for a small number of families from estranged fathers. Many of the mothers were depressed and anxious and quite worn down, and this impacted on their parenting with children, most of whom were of school age and indeed secondary school age, who were challenging both in and outside the home and who had been without boundaries.

For some of the children, school non-attendance was an issue, but this was often because of the child's anxiety about leaving their mother because of her depression and distress, and former domestic violence, with the child fearful of what would happen if they were not with their mother. However, the child might be resentful of the responsibility they were taking for their mother, with this expressed as anger within the home and towards the mother.

Several families also had older children who were now in their late teens or were young adults but still lived within the family home. They were often unemployed and had little money, with little routine or structure in their lives. They themselves could be quite dominant within the family home, seeking money from their mother, and bringing both boy and girl friends to the family home to sofa surf. Their presence was sometimes threatening for younger children as well as challenging for the mother.

It was the FRP's direct emotional and practical support for the mothers – such as undertaking cooking, cleaning or decorating beside them – which helped them to become less depressed and more confident and motivated. These were mothers who on their own and in isolation had needed to negotiate contact with multiple agencies and seek to tackle the impact of poverty and the task of parenting, often with little assistance. Although the intensiveness of the FRP engagement was demanding for the mothers, many welcomed and appreciated the friendship and structure from the FRP and no longer felt that they were on their own. This included FRP workers being beside the mothers as they had contact with other agencies and helping them to manage this contact and also getting other agencies (such as schools and housing) to be more responsive to the mother and family.

A major attribute of the FRP, alongside the intensiveness of its engagement with mothers and families, was that it was a 'team around the family'. Unlike other multi-professional and multiagency teams – such as community mental health teams (CMHTs), community teams for people with a learning disability (CTPLDS) and youth offending teams (YOTS) – here was a team that was not primarily focused on one issue or problem (e.g. the mental health or offending of one family member) but which, often through the deployment of a range of different workers with a range of expertise, sought to work with a number of family members, children and adults, on a range of different issues facing the family (e.g. housing, the mother's mental health, parenting, child protection concerns, children's behaviour and emotional turmoil).

It was also unlike a Team around the Child (TAC), which is usually a virtual team of separate workers about sharing information and assessments and coordinating action, but where the focus is on the child – not necessarily the whole family – and where there is no actual co-located team with a single manager.

The *big* message from this study is that the FRP is much valued by families (and especially the mothers who were interviewed) and by practitioners and managers in other agencies. Families were surprised by the intensity of the FRP engagement; some did not welcome how this was an additional demand within their lives, but more often the intensity became welcomed as it was found to be supportive as well as challenging.

Interviewees in other agencies particularly commented that the FRP engaged and communicated well with them and it was seen as value for money as it was making an impact on what had been particularly demanding families. Their main recommendation for change was to expand the FRP and increase the number of families with whom it worked.

However, because of the intensity of the FRP's work with families, especially the positive impact for mothers, how to help families sustain progress and not to leave mothers stranded on their own again with pressures and stresses is an issue. Welfare reform and greater poverty are likely to be ahead, which could easily overwhelm the mothers and families again, despite their changed parenting and enhanced motivation.

This is a limitation of the FRP and of the 'troubled families' model. It is separate and marginal to mainstream services. One lesson from this and other similar studies is that this may be a multiagency, multi-professional and intensive model to be mainstreamed. This would, of course, require more money, time and workers. It would also require a political and policy commitment to tackle distress, depression and disadvantage and not only 'trouble'. Although largely presented as being about 'control', the FRP service is as much about 'care'. It is challenging, and when necessary confrontational, but it is also concerned for families as well their impact on others. There are lessons here more generally for the development of social work and the reclaiming of the space for psychosocial, relationship-based practice and also for the organisation of family services.

References

Action for Children (2013) *Evaluation of Action for Children's Intensive Family Support Services*. London: Action for Children.

BBC (2011) 'England riots: Cameron to boost troubled-families plans.' *BBC Website* 15 August 2011. Available at www.bbc.co.uk/news/uk-politics-14527540, accessed on 17 October 2014.

Blair, T. (1995) *Leader's Speech*. Brighton: Labour Party Conference. Available at www.britishpoliticalspeech.org/speech-archive.htm?speech=201, accessed on 17 October 2014.

Cooper, J. (1983) *The Creation of the British Social Services 1962–1974*. London: Heinemann.

Department for Communities and Local Government (2012) *The Troubled Families Programme*. London: Department of Communities and Local Government. Available at www.communities.gov.uk/communities/troubledfamilies, accessed on 17 October 2014.

Department for Education (2011) *Monitoring and Evaluation of Family Intervention Services and Projects between February 2007 and March 2011*. London: Department for Education.

Dillane, J., Hill, M., Bannister, J. and Scott, S. (2001) *Evaluation of the Dundee Families Project*. Edinburgh: The Stationery Office.

Gregg, D. (2010) *Family Intervention Projects: A Classic Case of Policy-Based Evidence*. London: Centre for Crime and Justice Studies.

Hall, P. (1976) *Reforming the Welfare: The Politics of Change in the Personal Social Services*. London: Heinemann.

Levitas, R. (2012) 'There may be "trouble" ahead: what we know about those 120,000 "troubled" families.' *Poverty and Social Exclusion in the UK*. Policy Response Series No. 3. ESCRC: Swindon.

Murphy, D., Duggan, M. and Joseph, S.D. (2013) 'Relationship-based social work and its compatibility with the person-centred approach: principled versus instrumental perspectives.' *British Journal of Social Work 43*, 703–719.

Parr, S. (2009) 'Family intervention projects: a site of social work practice.' *British Journal of Social Work 39*, 1256–1273.

Ruch, G., Turney, D. and Ward, A. (2010) *Relationship-Based Social Work: Getting to the Heart of Practice*. London: Jessica Kingsley Publishers.

Rutter, M. and Madge, N. (1976) *Cycles of Disadvantage*. London: Heinemann.

Seebohm Committee (1968) *Report of the Committee on Local Authority and Allied Personal Social Services*. Cmnd 3701. London: HMSO.

Talbot, C. (2012) 'Trouble with troubled families research.' *Public Finance*, 19 July 2012. Available at http://opinion.publicfinance.co.uk/2012/07/trouble-with-troubled-families-research, accessed on 17 October 2014.

Thoburn, J., Cooper, N., Brandon, M. and Connelly, S. (2012) 'The place of "Think Family" approaches in child and family social work: messages from a process evaluation of an English Pathfinder service.' *Children and Youth Services Review 35*, 228–236.

Turner, F. (2009) 'Psychosocial Therapy.' In A. Roberts (ed.) *Social Workers' Desk Reference*. New York: Oxford University Press.

CHAPTER 7

International Perspectives

NIGEL HALL, KINGSTON UNIVERSITY

Taking a step back from the preoccupations of the debate in the UK, this chapter will look at policy and practice abroad. Research findings from the United States will be considered, but the chapter will also seek to think through the relevance of the concept of 'troubled families' cross-culturally by reviewing the international literature on family-oriented social work.

Introduction

While 'troubled families' may be a particularly UK concept, working with families in difficulty is naturally the focus of social workers' attention all over the world. In considering how an international perspective might provide some alternative perspectives that could inform the debate of how best to work with troubled families, this chapter will initially examine perspectives drawn from the developing (or 'non-Western') world, then return to the developed (or 'Western') world. It is recognised that this distinction is not particularly helpful, as many countries feature elements of both 'worlds' – i.e. marginalised poor communities alongside privileged and richer elite groups, so there may be some interweaving. However there are 'lessons' to be learnt from even very dissimilar situations and this chapter will consider selected examples of work with families from countries as diverse as Vietnam, the Maldives, Zimbabwe, South Africa, Spain, Jamaica, New Zealand, Guatemala,

Chile, Argentina, the United States, Denmark and the Netherlands. Key issues concern the place of the family in the modern world, particularly the loss of the extended family and its support systems, the pressures on families to survive in a time of austerity, the impact of disease, conflict and migration and the need to try to bring families back together where they have become fragmented to help its members, while helping prevent problems arising in the first place.

The current *Global Definition of Social Work* states that 'Principles of social justice, human rights, collective responsibility and respect for diversities are central to social work' (IFSW 2014). This has profound implications for thinking through what diversities really mean, and in the context of working with families this comprises many different situations – from the constituent individuals to the broader society – and working in different social, political and cultural contexts. Although social work's origins are in Europe and America and the profession has spread around the world, Payne and Askeland (2008) point out that we need to question whether Western models of social work practice and organisation are universal. Their answer is that although this may provide something of a framework for understanding social work, different cultural assumptions and social needs require different approaches to social work and that 'a worldwide view of social work might be richer if it included ideas from other perceptions in non-Western countries' (Payne and Askeland 2008, p.4). Of course, Western countries themselves differ widely in the way they deal with social problems, so there are certainly a variety of approaches to draw on. Dealing with 'troubled families', or working with families with multiple social problems, is one such area, with diverse and even conflicting approaches manifest.

Breakdown of the extended family

Cox and Pawar (2006) point out how important the family is in the developing world context and suggest several reasons why this is the case: caring services are located in the household; the household economy is very important, particularly where social safety nets are lacking; the provision of health and education relies very much on the cooperation of the family, especially in relation to females and children; and it is the family unit that is most affected when things go wrong. This is often not the case today however where the family is often under severe stress. As Cox and Pawar (2006, p.139) note: 'All local workers, however, will always need to bear in mind the roles of the family, the pressures on families in a specific context, and the likely implications for families of any activities undertaken locally.'

The nature and form of the family is something that is very changeable. As Lawrence *et al.* (2009) note, there is the distinction between the nuclear family – more common in Western societies – and the extended family – much more significant in non-Western societies – which often consists of three generations, with aunts, uncles and cousins often sharing the same home or living in close proximity to each other. Such extended families were able to meet the practical, social and emotional needs of family members, provided constraints and opportunities for those members and contributed to creating stable societies. This is still the case to some extent, but in many ways the role of the family has been significantly weakened by a variety of factors.

In much of the developing world, families are experiencing rapid social change, dire poverty and often the spread of infectious diseases. Consequently, they are in a continuous state of vulnerability. In addition, socioeconomic changes that might leave them in a precarious situation, such as the push factors for migration, either to seek work or due to instability of some type are commonplace, while the 'nuclearisation' of families has diminished the role of the extended family and its role as a buffer against hardship and a source of social security. In this situation most families are 'troubled', mainly by the daily struggle to survive. Increasing numbers of poor families and orphaned children have to survive on their own with no Government safety net, such as might exist in Western countries. This is why in these countries social work needs to have more of a social developmental role and social work with families is very much linked to this.

Need for a social developmental role

Laird (2008) points out that the basic tenet of a developmental approach is to move towards expanding people's capabilities while improving their socioeconomic circumstances and notes that the incorporation of a strengths perspective is therefore a crucial component of developmental social work. The interventions employed to address the problems of disadvantaged families will comprise activities such as micro-financing, vocational training, functional literacy, school sponsorship, intermediate technology transfer and community-based approaches, many of which will be provided through the NGO (non-governmental organisation) sector, often by social workers or community development workers. In focusing on social work practice in sub-Saharan Africa Laird (2008, p.147) notes that the literature reveals that some of the most effective strategies are built around:

> reciprocal exchanges of resources within communities, the pooling of community resources as a whole, the intricate domestic and economic collaboration of intergenerational households, and the diversification of livelihoods.

Developing appropriate forms of social work

Helping families in resource-poor situations where poverty is commonplace means supporting and promoting reciprocal relationships, building on traditional coping strategies and developing additional adaptations in support of activity to improve living standards. Hugman (2010) for example examines how social workers assist families facing difficulties of various kinds in Vietnam. He profiles the work of the child protection service of UNICEF Vietnam to develop 'barefoot social workers' in remote areas. In this approach, female members of local communities are recruited and given short-course training in basic social work concepts and methods. They are then employed on a part-time basis to provide advice and counselling to families in their local communities who are experiencing multiple difficulties. These women may provide direct assistance, for example in taking care of a child in order to give a mother with mental health problems some respite, providing psychosocial support and links to formal services to families facing issues with extreme poverty or with family members who may have HIV.

Hugman points out that in recent years a national study was undertaken to examine the need for a formal social work profession in Vietnam (UNICEF Vietnam/Ministry of Labour, Invalids and Social Affairs (MOLISA) 2007). This study concluded that there was a substantive need for social services in the areas of families facing multiple difficulties (including where child abuse and domestic violence are prevalent), where there are mental health issues, disabled and older people requiring support, the social impacts of prostitution, drug misuse, HIV/AIDS and crime. This study and the developmental work that extended from it explicitly recognised that importance of developing a form of social work appropriate for Vietnam – seen as 'social work with Vietnamese characteristics'. Hugman notes that the role of university-trained social workers in the next decade is likely to be one where they are able to deal:

> ...with complex situations, supervising and supporting local practitioners in the wards and communes and to be able to contribute through more senior roles in management, research and policy development. (Hugman 2010, p.142)

At the same time, it is seen as important to develop appropriate education and training materials that are suitable for Vietnam and there is now a process in place to focus not only on appropriate direct practice, but also to give attention to organisational and educational matters and gear this towards the current needs of families and the community more generally. The example of Vietnam demonstrates the key features of the development of more relevant models of social work that were identified by Midgley (1981) in his landmark study of social work in the developing world (i.e. his concerns over 'professional imperialism') as being more appropriate in attempting to progress beyond neo-colonialism.

Listening to the family and its concerns

Hussain *et al.* (2012) consider how a team of social workers in the Maldives has assisted families in extreme difficulty through the Child and Family Protection Service (CFPS) of the Ministry for Health and Family. They point out that although the country has largely benefited from tourism-based development, many families in the islands face significant problems and consequently the vulnerabilities of families – especially with regard to children and adolescents – have increased. This is partly due to family break-up, with some moving to resort islands looking for work, and also due to families migrating in order for children to attend better schools largely concentrated in urban areas. Often fathers do not see their families for years at a time. The authors explain how local community members were mobilised, given minimal training on issues such as child safety and advice on accessing support to address domestic violence and then worked closely with family members. Through listening carefully to the concerns of community members, proving resources to meet these concerns, by delivering these in a respectful and gender-sensitive ways in a very patriarchal society:

> Communities began to accept that they had to take some responsibility in the child protection process and had an important role to play in assisting families that are in difficult circumstances... It is vital that the social services continue to have energetic and creative leaders [who are] actively committed. (Hussain *et al.* 2012, p.111)

This approach was modelled from Tanzania's 'barefoot health workers' scheme in the 1970s to deliver basic health services to a great number of people.

Making men responsible for families

'Troubled families' is a description that could be applied to families in many developing countries, another example being Zimbabwe in sub-Saharan Africa. Here 14 per cent of Zimbabweans live with

HIV and AIDS, one of the highest prevalence rates in the world. While the global HIV/AIDS incidence is declining, rates of new infections remain very high in many sub-Saharan Africa countries. In Zimbabwe out of 1,400,000 people infected (a 14.7% prevalence rate), 180,000 are children under 14 years of age (UNAIDS 2014). The disease therefore remains the most striking public health issue in the country. Children whose parents are HIV-positive face multiple vulnerabilities, such as becoming infected themselves, risking losing parental care and being subject to social discrimination and neglect, while in many cases where parents are deceased, siblings are cared for in child-headed households or by ageing grandparents. The epidemic has devastated families here, but key initiatives pioneered through NGOs have been able to help in strengthening families. One interesting initiative carried out through a southern Africa regional NGO (SAfAIDS) was to encourage men to become more considerate and sexually responsible through promoting public education campaigns in beer halls, for example, and developing AIDS champions in the community. Improving circumstances for families has implications for men in relation to taking more responsibility for their own families:

> This means society as a whole must change. Political and community leaders should recognise the role of men in the epidemic, change their own behaviour and encourage policies that support change. Religious leaders must recognise and respond to all the different factors influencing men's behaviour and the media can raise awareness of the role of men and the need for men to change. (SAfAIDS, PANOS, UNAIDS 2001, p.25)

Strengthening families

Families are likely to need considerable help to manage in these adverse circumstances. The work of SOS Children's Villages in Zimbabwe is notable through their SOS Family Strengthening Programmes. The programmes enable children who are at risk of losing parental care to grow up within a caring family environment. When children can no longer stay with their families, they are cared for by their SOS mothers in one of the SOS families in three different locations in the country, by providing day care, education and vocational training. Since 2003, Family Strengthening Programmes have offered access to essential services for children's development and supporting families to protect and care for their children. The programmes reach out to over 3000 children a year and provide them and their families with food, school fees, basic medical treatment, counselling and psychosocial support (see SOS Children's Villages 2014). This is consistent with research findings from Lyons, Manion and Carlsen (2006) who point out how social professionals can strengthen the coping capacity of families by providing direct financial assistance, home visits, food and nutritional support and waiving of school fees.

Working towards radical transformation

Developmental social work is emerging as a new paradigm in international social work that seeks to infuse social developmental theory and practice into social work processes (Midgley and Conley 2010). Social work and social development are professional disciplines that are starting to be fused together, significantly at the level of the 'Global Agenda' mentioned later. A good example of this can be found in South Africa. Patel and Hochfeld (2013) point out that this country is unique in that the developmental approach to social welfare and social work was adopted as national government policy in 1997 after the collapse of apartheid, and their view is that the country is to be commended for an ambitious and progressive developmental welfare policy. However they remain critical of the piecemeal, fragmented and often contradictory basket of service delivery that so often fails service users (Patel and Hochfeld 2013, p.700). While this may be partly due to government priorities, there is also concern that families are affected in a detrimental way by the marketisation of policies on the delivery of social work services in contemporary South Africa. In an article by student social workers in South Africa the point is made that practitioners can no longer be satisfied with merely mitigating the negative effects of poverty, unemployment and inequality in practice when many of these problems are associated with neoliberal policies:

> The challenge however lies not just in social workers having to make critical choices to reposition themselves but also to critically reflect on their roles if they are to make a difference and address the needs of the most vulnerable and marginalised sectors of the population. (Raniga and Zelnick 2014, p.394)

Raniga and Zelnick (2014) suggest that what is required is a radical transformation of the welfare system and changes in the socio-structural and economic system that disadvantage both social workers and service users. The implication of this is that it is the macro-economic factors that propel families into destitution and poverty and which are behind social pathology, and unless this is dealt with, social work intervention is always going to be at the level of amelioration and 'patching up' of problems.

Global Agenda for Social Work and Social Development

It is worth mentioning at this stage the Global Agenda for Social Work and Social Development, an initiative that in 2010 stemmed from the three main global bodies representing social workers – the International Federation of Social Workers (IFSW), the International Association of Schools of Social Work (IASSW), and the International Council on Social Welfare (ICSW). This Agenda is seen as a basis for advocacy with regional and global bodies, including the United Nations, and as a way of demonstrating professional coherence, solidarity and credibility (Jones and Truell 2012). As part of this initiative, a Global Observatory is monitoring social work practice around the world, linked to a thematic topic – it is currently promoting social and economic equalities. An example of positive practice in working strategically on behalf of disadvantaged families is provided by Consejo, the General Council of Social Workers of Spain. The Council launched a campaign in 2012 called Marea Naranja (Orange Wave), which brings together citizens, social workers and other professionals. Social workers wear orange T-shirts to work every Friday and there is a nationwide programme of activities working with local communities and families in difficulty who campaign to challenge service reductions and uphold the social rights of citizens (IASSW, ICSW, IFSW 2014).

Countering community and family violence

Inequalities, social dislocation, drug abuse and the breakdown of family structure are the consequences of not dealing with some of these macro-social and systemic issues. This may lead to violence and the collapse of the normative standards that traditionally held families together. An example of community violence that spiralled out of control affecting and disrupting families can be found in Jamaica – a country that has the unfortunate distinction of most homicides per population. This has been brought about by a variety of factors – a harsh economic climate, poverty, inequality and ruthless political culture. As Levy (2012) reports, the predominant single parent nature of the family in Jamaica that worked well with a strong supportive extended family is now a thing of the past with nearly half of single parent household heads away working or having migrated in search of work a key feature. Levy reports on an initiative called the Peace Management Institute (PMI), a state and civil society alliance formed in 2002 by the Minister of National Security with the blessing of the two main political parties. For the first time, the state employed social workers and adopted applied social measures to reduce community violence. A PMI activist board (which has representatives of the two main political parties, ministers of religion, university lecturers and civil society members) takes a hands-on approach in working with the families and communities affected:

> In the PMI approach, board members and staff simply walk into a community rocked by war (violence) and engage the young shottas (shooters) in conversation, listening carefully to

each side... While this process is going forward, an auxiliary team of pastors and psychologists organised by a PMI staff person counsels those traumatised by the violent deaths of family members or close friends. (Levy 2012, p.168–169)

Engaging in conversation, not lecturing but listening, winning the trust of gang members and working with their families are key elements to this approach.

An even more extreme version of family breakdown and violence can be found in the Democratic Republic of the Congo (DRC) where sexual violence and rape are endemic in a conflict that led to the deaths of more than five million people in the 20 years since the war began in that region and where sexual assault has become so widespread that an estimated 48 Congolese women are raped every hour. While this personifies the complete breakdown of social norms, efforts continue by survivors to rebuild their shattered personal and family lives – for example the film *Seeds of Hope* follows Masika Katsuva, a rape survivor devoted to helping other survivors restore their sense of security, dignity and self-worth through farming and rebuild their family and community lives (see Pulitzer Centre 2014).

Involving family and community

Working with families should mean working with them in a respectful dialogue. Historically, post-colonial states have been subject to Eurocentric approaches that undermined their families and tribes – such as taking children for the purposes of adoption, which took place in the 19th and early 20th centuries in many developing countries. Although this has been the subject of official apologies from Western leaders, the statuses of many indigenous peoples have been dire in the extreme.

This has been exacerbated in countries like New Zealand, where many state-funded social services have been withdrawn and the third sector has been asked to fill the gaps created. The result has been a fragmentation of service delivery, particularly in the area of at-risk children, young people and families. In order to deal with this and move forward, in the tradition of bi-culturalism (between the indigenous Maori and the White settler (Pakeha) community), major reforms to the child welfare and youth justice systems were made (under the Strengthening Families Initiative) and New Zealand became the first nation to legislate Family Group Conferencing (FGC) in working with families and children, which has since been extended to many countries.

FGC is an international success story in dealing with complex family dynamics. Rotabi *et al.* (2012) indicate how FGC encourages participation by different sides of the family in Norway, can be carried out safely even in situations of domestic violence in the United States and Canada and generates plans reflecting children's cultural background and families' ethic of caring for their young relatives in both the United Stated and the UK. These authors also report on its success in the Marshall Islands and consider how FGC could be used in Guatemala. Within Guatemala, FGC is taught within the curriculum of the National University and is referred to in Spanish as auto-ayuda-familiar, i.e. family self-help groups. As Rotabi *et al.* (2012, p.411) point out:

> Students learn how to bring family members together to find a commonly agreed-upon solution to an identified problem affecting the family. The social worker is responsible for overseeing the orientation, assessment and support of the family.

The strength of FGC is its flexibility and the fact that it can be adapted to suit local cultures and bring in the extended family to support families in crisis.

A shift to family-centred practice under New Zealand's Strengthening Families Initiative, with its emphasis on collaborative partnerships as the means to deliver services to multiple needs families, was predicated on New Zealand's Children, Young Persons and Their Families Act of 1989 and has been held up internationally as a model of excellent practice. Research conducted by McKenzie, Kelliher and Henderson (2001) indicated that this model is being used to deal with complex problem issues, often with families that have limited familial and/or social supports and advocacy to call upon.

This research also demonstrated that greater emphasis should be based on a neutral facilitator chairing the meetings to ensure that the voice of the family is not lost, that sufficient information is provided on the process involved, that more attention is given to dealing with the complexity of the problems faced by the families and that more support is needed for the parents rather than just the children. While some parents felt they were not supported enough, nearly 90 per cent still indicated the relationships they had with the agencies and professionals involved changed positively during the Strengthening Families process. It was interesting to note that the role of grandparents was seen to be important.

Empowering families

While New Zealand dealt with issues of marginalisation and discrimination through involving the wider family and community, in other developing parts of the world these inequalities were very evident and of concern to social workers practising there. Extreme poverty has been an issue that social workers have grappled with in Latin America, where the profession's roots can be traced back to the early twentieth century in Chile, where the first school of social work was created in 1925. Social work education and practice has evolved through several transitions, initially from an effort to reduce poverty by teaching appropriate work ethics to the poor, but later denounced as a means of creating an active labour class to support capitalism and sustain the ruling class. Following a period in the 1950s when social work became heavily influenced by individualistic developments in the United States, the profession underwent what came to be known as the 'reconceptualization process', which challenged the remedial nature of social work and emphasised how marginalised groups were exploited and oppressed. Theories that guided this thinking, and which are still very prominent within Latin American social work, were liberation theology, 'conscientization' and Marxist ideology, among others, where social workers believed that social work should bring social change to oppressive structures.

Latin American social workers would not frame the situation as working with 'difficult' or 'troubled' families and would be more likely to view them as victims and to look to where support could be found (labour unions, social movements, etc.), and where action could be taken through grassroots organisations to address the socio-political and economic realities of the marginalised – and counter what they would see as the impact of neoliberal policies on vulnerable sectors of society. The Latino culture has a strong orientation towards embracing older adults within the family, but this is often not possible today due to the harsh economic circumstances families face. However, social workers have helped families survive the financial crisis through the creation of communal cooperatives (e.g. the cartoneros movement in Argentina, see Queiro-Tajalli 2012).

Family-based/centred services and family practice

In the United States, working with troubled families tends to connote a more clinical and therapeutic approach to family problems. There has always been a strong family orientation in social work practice in the United States, originally stemming from the work of the Charity Organisation Society and Settlement Movement, which had emphasised a systemic approach where the family was seen within the broader social environment. However the psychoanalytic movement in the early twentieth century diverted attention from the family and led to the individualisation of social problems, and this remained the pre-eminent social work strategy for many decades.

The return to the family as a primary focus of attention in direct practice occurred in the 1950s and 1960s with a greater focus on urban America and the plight of families entrapped within the public welfare system. Rasheed and Rasheed (2011, p.183) point out:

These families more often than not were not only faced with poverty but also with issues of delinquency, neglect and severe health problems. These families, referred to as the 'multiproblem families', garnered the concern of many social scientists.

The interdisciplinary family therapy movement also emerged at this time and this together with systemic approaches infused social work practice with a range of interventions with families. In the United States a distinction is often made between 'family-based' or 'family-centred' social work versus 'family practice' (Collins, Jordan and Coleman 1999).

Family-based/centred services comprise a range of activities such as case management, counselling/therapy, education, skill-building, advocacy and provision of direct services (such as housing, food or clothes). Family practice connotes a more direct clinical/therapeutic approach to family problems as well as broader systemic factors impacting family life. An example here might be to help families learn more effective problem-solving skills in order to reduce the number of crises and increase the likelihood of supportive rather than destructive family interactions.

Clark and Woods-Waller (2006) point out that the mission of the profession in the United States is based on a set of core values, including: service; social justice; dignity and worth of the person; importance of human relationships; integrity; and competence. As noted by Watkins, Jennisen and Lundy (2012), the roles and responsibilities of social workers in the United States has grown over time and now includes culturally and ethnically diverse populations and services directed at demographically varied populations. They note that the clear trend in social work practice has been the continued privatisation of services and although social work services are in even greater demand, they are also often decreased in attempts to reduce expenditures, in both the private and public sectors. So although there is enormous need for family-oriented work, the fragmentation of social work itself and the encroachment of other professions and quasi-professions into the social work domain creates challenges for the future.

New ways of working can develop from this inter-professional approach. In Rochester, New York, for example, the Police Department utilises a model called FACIT – the Family and Crisis Intervention Team, which consists of civilian social workers and counsellors employed by the police department, who respond to cases involving domestic disputes, mental health issues, alcohol and substance misuse, landlord–tenant problems, child abuse, juvenile delinquency and the needs of the elderly. The unit is assigned work with cases of crimes against children and referrals for juvenile diversion from the Family Court System.

Family preservation programmes

Many states in the United States operate 'family preservation' programmes, which use a particular model of service delivery that underscores the importance of restoring families to safe levels of functioning. As a service model, family preservation programmes share common features including intensive services delivered over a relatively short period of time, individualised to a family's needs and offered in the family home or community – under the Family Support and Preservation Act (1993). There was a backlash to this in the 1990s following media stories of children who suffered serious and sometimes fatal injuries in difficult families, with critics attacking family preservation services as preserving families at the expense of child safety, and later a much stronger emphasis was placed on child safety through the Adoption and Safe Families Act (ASWFA) in 1997. Much of what is now termed 'family-centred practice' was first embodied in the family preservation movement (Gelles 2001). Caseloads are typically small so that the worker can be easily accessible to the family, and they are often available 24 hours a day for emergencies and crisis intervention. The period of time for service delivery varies from one month to several months depending on the model and is time limited in order to restore family functioning as soon as possible. Many family preservation programmes now work closely with community groups and have helped broaden the definition of family by including extended family members and natural helping networks. Further examples of family practice can be noted.

Family to Family initiative

Also in the United States, Midgley and Conley (2010) report on the Family to Family initiative, sponsored by The Annie E. Casey Foundation that in a similar way to FGC harnesses communities' interests in protecting their children. This Foundation encourages partnerships with extended families and communities to protect children and support families, working with both natural and foster families to keep children in their local community. Beginning with five states and three additional counties in 1993, the initiative had spread to 18 states and more than 80 sites across the United States by 2009, although the project itself has now ceased.

> For Family to Family to be successful, the community has to be included as a real partner, right from the start. Strong relationships with the community will help sustain changes and can help the agency in the face of various kinds of pressure – for example, from the media or the courts. This means reaching out to community leaders to involve them in the planning process – from creating the vision to thinking with you about how the work of the agency might need to change. (The Annie E. Casey Foundation 2001, p.18)

The main point of Family to Family was enabling more children to stay within their neighbourhoods of origin and experience a greater sense of stability and community.

Another strategy that extended from this initiative is Team Decision Making, a process that invites community and extended family involvement in case planning for children.

Pedagogic approaches

A similar approach can be found in Denmark where the Danish Government has, through its social development programme, put a great emphasis on prevention strategies in supporting families with serious difficulties, such as those where parents are affected by drug and alcohol abuse. Hatton (2006) reports that there has been a significant reduction in the number of children being removed from home in the last few decades, and where this decision is made under their Social Assistance Act, it is done so by a social committee in each locality, consisting of three municipal politicians, one judge and one psychologist – contrasting sharply with the British and Irish systems, where the decision is made by the courts. As noted by the Ministry of Social Affairs (1995, p.66):

> It remains the guiding principle that preventative social measures in Denmark be directed towards supporting the family, in such a way as to provide optimum conditions for the child's growth and development.

Van Ewijk (2010) also comments on the social care system in Denmark, where he notes that Danish experts prefer to speak about pedagogy instead of care and how this pedagogical perspective connects childcare, elderly care, care for the disabled, youth care, community care and community development (see Cameron and Moss 2007). Social pedagogy is drawn from the concept of education in its widest sense and attempts to deal with problems in a holistic way. The Danish pedagogic approach in social work, the development of community projects and a strong emphasis on prevention have led to policies that can support families in difficulty, although resource constraints obviously have affected the work of voluntary organisations.

As Lyons, Manion and Carlsen (2006) and Lyons et al. (2012) observe, at the core of the pedagogical relationship are notions of equality and respect and the eradication of unequal power relations. It draws on Freirian ideas about 'conscientization' (Freire 1972), particularly where Freire talks about the need for dialogue, critical thinking and developing an awareness of oppressive situations that prevent citizens from engaging constructively in the world – as through adverse circumstances, poverty and discrimination they have been forced into a 'culture of silence' where they cannot speak up for themselves.

Multi-agencies together in promoting change

Van der Laan (2000) considers how the marketisation of social work is helping to transform social work in the Netherlands, and how this has impacted on work with multi-problem families. He mentions how, given an increase in applications for material assistance, some generic social work agencies decided to devote extra attention to concrete aid, especially in the cities of Utrecht and The Hague. Cooperative projects were set up relating to case management, debt management, problems families and chronic psychiatric patients. Some projects, for example those set up for families who have been evicted from their homes as a result of nuisance or indebtedness, now include their signing a contract with social work and with regard to housing. Counselling would go along with the offer of housing or debt reconciliation – i.e. with the latter example, only if they opt for counselling does the project negotiate with their creditors to freeze or reschedule their debts while they receive counselling. In this way the process is similar to the family practice initiative within the United States.

While this may seem a successful approach to working with 'difficult' individuals and families, Van de Laan (2000, p.100) feels that social work is in new territory here and needs to make some key choices regarding direction:

> Should social work be willing to conceive social problems, such as crime, nuisance, debt, disablement and unemployment, in terms of behavioural change, and to use its professional power to steer clients towards the changes prescribed by the commissioning authorities?

He feels that a concerted effort is needed for social workers to preserve their professional standards, between the demands of their clients and the financial incentives provided by the commissioning institutions.

Conclusion

This chapter has attempted to consider the relevance of the concept of 'troubled families' cross-culturally by reviewing some key international literature on family-oriented social work in different parts of the world. While there are a variety of approaches to working with families, several major themes stand out – the need to rebuild families in the wake of the loss of the extended family, the changing concept or definition of social work to include ideas of social development, where work with families and communities are placed centre stage, the deployment of para-professionals listening closely to the concerns of family members and considering the role of men in families and helping them to take more responsibility, in parts of the world where this is appropriate.

Strengthening families through various programmes, both governmental and non-governmental, is important, but so is considering more radical measures aimed at reducing social and economic disparities and finding ways to counter community and intra-family violence. Involving the family is key to much of this and family-centred or family-based practice, where the family and its constituent members are fully involved and empowered, are key aspirations. Social workers also need to consider how they can nurture and support families and build on prevention programmes to stop problems from escalating and becoming more serious.

Finally, social workers need to consider how they can work with other agencies to promote behavioural change, where this is seen to be needed, and how this relates to their own professional values.

References

Cameron, C. and Moss, P. (2007) *Care Work in Europe: Current Understandings and Future Directions.* London: Routledge.

Clark, E.J. and Woods-Waller, G. (2006) 'Improving the Profession. Changing Perceptions – Social Work in the USA.' In N. Hall (ed.) (2006) *Social Work: Making a World of Difference. Social Work Around the World IV.* Oslo: International Federation of Social Workers (IFSW) and Fafo, Norway.

Collins, D., Jordan, C. and Coleman, H. (1999) *An Introduction to Family Social Work.* Itasca, IL: FE Peacock.

Cox, D. and Pawar, M. (2006) *International Social Work: Issues, Strategies and Programs*. London: Sage Publications.

Freire, P. (1972) *Pedagogy of the Oppressed*. Harmondsworth: Penguin.

Gelles, R.J. (2001) 'Family Preservation and Reunification: How Effective a Social Policy?' In S.O. White (ed.) *Handbook of Youth and Justice*. New York: Kluwer Academic/Plenum Publishers. Available at: www.sp2.upenn.edu/onechild/research/family_preservation.pdf, accessed on 29 June 2014.

Hatton, K. (2006) 'Europe and the Undergraduate Programme.' In K. Lyons and S. Lawrence (eds) *Social Work in Europe: Educating for Change*. Birmingham: BASW, Venture Press.

Hugman, R. (2010) *Understanding International Social Work: A Critical Analysis*. Basingstoke: Palgrave Macmillan.

Hussain, A., Agleem, M., Ali, M. and O'Dempsey, M. (2012) 'Developing Child Protection Groups in Remote Island Communities of the Maldives.' In N. Hall (ed.) (2012) *Social Work Around the World V: Building the Global Agenda for Social Work and Social Development*. Berne: IFSW.

IFSW (2014) *Global Definition of Social Work*. Berne: IFSW. Available at http://ifsw.org/policies/definition-of-social-work/, accessed on 28 November 2014.

IASSW, ICSW, IFSW (2014) *Global Agenda for Social Work and Social Development First Report 2014: Promoting Social and Economic Equalities*. London: Sage.

Jones, D. and Truell, R. (2012) 'The Global Agenda for Social Work and Social Development: a place to link together and be effective in a globalised world.' *International Social Work 55*, 4, 454–472.

Laird, S.E. (2008) 'Social work practice to support survival strategies in Sub-Saharan Africa.' *British Journal of Social Work 38*, 135–151.

Lawrence, S., Lyons, K., Simpson, G. and Huegler, N. (2009) *Introducing International Social Work*. Exeter: Learning Matters.

Levy, H. (2012) 'Community Violence.' In L.M. Healy and R.J. Link (eds) *Handbook on International Social Work*. London: Oxford University Press.

Lyons, J., Hokenstad, T., Pawar, M., Huegler, N. and Hall, N. (eds) (2012) *The Sage Handbook of International Social Work*. London: Sage.

Lyons, K., Manion, K. and Carlsen, M. (2006) *International Perspectives on Social Work: Global Conditions and Local Practice*. Basingstoke: Palgrave Macmillan.

McKenzie, M., Kelliher, M. and Henderson, M. (2001) 'The shift to family-centred practice in social work: family voice in evaluation of the Strengthening Families initiative.' *Aotearoa New Zealand Association of Social Workers Social Work Review XIII*, 1, 13–19.

Midgley, J. (1981) *Professional Imperialism*. London: Heinemann.

Midgley, J. and Conley, A. (2010) *Social Work and Social Development: Theories and Skills for Developmental Social Work*. New York: Oxford University Press.

Ministry of Social Affairs (1995) *Report on the Seminar on Transfer of Know-how and Good Practice from Poverty*. Copenhagen: Ministry of Social Affairs.

Patel, L. and Hochfeld, T. (2013) 'Developmental social work in South Africa: translating policy.' *International Social Work 56*, 5, 690–704.

Payne, M. and Askeland, G.A. (2008) *Globalization and International Social Work: Postmodern Change and Challenge.* Farnham: Ashgate.

Pulitzer Centre (2014) '*Seeds of Hope' Screening Linked to Global Summit to End Sexual Violence in Conflict.* Washington, DC: Pulitzer Centre. Available at http://pulitzercenter.org/event/seeds-hope-screening-global-summit-end-sexual-violence-rape-weapon-war-congo, accessed on 17 October 2014.

Queiro-Tajalli, I. (2012) 'Social Work in Latin America.' In L.M. Healy and R.J. Link (eds) *Handbook on International Social Work.* London: Oxford University Press.

Raniga, T. and Zelnick, J. (2014) 'Social policy education for change: South African student perspectives on the Global Agenda for Social Work and Social Development.' *International Social Work 57*, 4, 386–397.

Rasheed, M.N. and Rasheed J.M. (2011) 'Family: Practice Interventions.' In T. Mizrahi and L. Davis (eds) *Encyclopedia of Social Work: 20th edition Volume 2.* New York: Oxford University Press.

Rotabi, K.S., Pennell, J., Roby, J.L. and Bunkers, K.M. (2012) 'Family group conferencing as a culturally adaptable intervention: reforming intercountry adoption in Guatemala.' *International Social Work 55*, 3, 402–416.

SAfAIDS, PANOS, UNAIDS (2001) *Men and HIV in Zimbabwe.* Ruwa: SAfAIDS, PANOS, UNAIDS.

SOS Children's Villages (2014) *SOS Children in Zimbabwe.* Available at www.soschildrensvillages.org.uk/sponsor-a-child/africa/zimbabwe?gclid=CMHh4_Cz274CFS3HtAodHQQAzA, accessed on 17 October 2014. Highlands/Harare, Zimbabwe: SOS Children's Villages

The Annie E. Casey Foundation (2001) *Family to Family: Tools for Re-building Foster Care. Lessons Learned.* Available at www.aecf.org/m/resourcedoc/aecf-F2FLessonsLearned-2001.pdf, accessed on 27 November 2014. Baltimore, MD: The Annie E. Casey Foundation.

UNAIDS (2014) *Zimbabwe – HIV and AIDS estimates.* Available at www.unaids.org/en/regionscountries/countries/zimbabwe, accessed on 17 October 2014.Geneva: UNAIDS.

UNICEF Vietnam/Ministry of Labour, Invalids and Social Affairs (MOLISA) (2007) *Professional Social Work in Vietnam: A Strategic Framework.* Hanoi: UNICEF Vietnam/MOLISA.

Van der Laan, G. (2000) 'Social Work in the Netherlands.' In A. Adams, P. Erath and S. Shardlow (2000) *Fundamentals of Social Work in Selected European Countries.* Lyme Regis: Russell House Publishing.

Van Ewijk, H. (2010) *European Social Policy and Social Work: Citizenship-based Social Work.* London: Routledge.

Watkins, J., Jennisen, T. and Lundy, C. (2012) 'Community Violence.' In L.M. Healy and R.J. Link (eds) *Handbook on International Social Work.* London: Oxford University Press.

CONTRIBUTORS

Dr Ian Byford worked for over 20 years as a social worker and social work manager, and is about to celebrate another 20 years as a social work lecturer. He has a particular interest in research ethics, and has served on and chaired a University research ethics committee. His current research is an evaluation of public health services in a local authority.

Keith Davies BA, MSc, MRes is Associate Professor at Kingston University. He has many years of experience working with 'troubled families', largely as a practitioner in criminal justice. Keith has had articles published in *The Probation Journal, The Journal of Social Work Education* and the *British Journal of Community Justice*.

Nigel Hall is the MA in Advanced Social Work Course Director at Kingston University. He is Senior Lecturer in the School of Social Work and has practical and academic experience in social work in the UK and Zimbabwe. He has voluntary executive roles with the International Federation of Social Workers (IFSW) and has authored and edited a variety of publications. His special areas of interest include adult social care and international social work.

Professor Carol Hayden researches children and families with multiple problems. Within this broad area she has several key specialism that include: children who are excluded or disaffected from school; children in the care system; Restorative Justice approaches as they relate to children; victimisation and children; children missing from home or care; addressing the needs of children who present highly problematic behaviour in different contexts (particularly in care and in schools).

David Holmes CBE LLB LLM has been Chief Executive of Family Action since 2013, a national charity providing more than 120 services across England to children and families including more than 50 family support services. He was previously Chief Executive of the British Association for Adoption and Fostering (2006-13). David has senior management experience in children's services in the voluntary sector, local government and central government and began his career as a solicitor in private practice. David is currently Chair of Children England, Chair of Naomi House (a children's hospice group) and Chair of the End Child Poverty campaign. David was awarded a CBE for Services to Children and Families in the New Year Honours 2014.

Craig Jenkins is a professional researcher. He has researched a variety of criminological issues including: prison resettlement; sport based crime prevention; Police technologies; social policy. He has now began to specialise in families with multiple complex needs in relation to the Troubled Families Programme.

Dr Ray Jones is professor of social work at Kingston University and St George's, University of London, and is a registered social worker. From 1992 to 2006 he was director of social services in Wiltshire. He was the first chief executive of the Social Care Institute for Excellence, and has been deputy chair and chair of the British Association of Social Workers. He is chair of the charity which organises 'The Social Worker of the Year Awards'. He has led inquiries following the deaths of children and adults, from 2009 to 2013 was chair of Bristol's Safeguarding Children Board, and he has overseen child protection improvement in Salford, Torbay, the Isle of Wight, Sandwell and Devon. His most recent book, *The Story of Baby P: Setting the Record Straight*, was published in July 2014, and he is a frequent media contributor, commentator and columnist.

Anna Matczak is a Doctoral Researcher at the Department of Sociology, London School of Economics and Political Science (LSE). She holds a MSc in Social Policy (Research) from the LSE and a MA in Social Policy from the University of Warsaw. Prior to beginning her Ph.D. she was working as a Researcher at Kingston University & St George's University of London and Anglia Ruskin University. She is also a qualified court and police interpreter. Her research interests engage with restorative justice, domestic violence, attitudinal research on crime and punishment, penal policies in Central and Eastern European countries. She tweets @MatczakAnia.

Dr Sadie Parr is a research fellow at the Centre for Regional, Economic and Social Research, Sheffield Hallam University. Her main research interests lie broadly within the fields of family and parenting policy, crime control and community safety. She has researched and published widely on the role of family interventions in the governance of anti-social behaviour.

June Thoburn, CBE, LittD, MSW is an Emeritus Professor of Social Work and member of the Centre For Research on Children and Families at the University of East Anglia, Norwich, England. She worked in local authority social work in England and Canada before joining UEA in 1979. Her teaching and research have encompassed family support and child protection services for families in the community and services for children in care or placed for adoption.

SUBJECT INDEX

adult offending 49
advocacy support 57, 90, 173
anti-social behaviour (ASB)
  effect of projects 21–2, 39
  emphasis on, in PBR 12–13
  goal of reducing 97, 101
  political interest in 13, 19–20, 74,
    124–5
  as TFP criterion 31, 32, 42, 53,
    100
  traditional forms of social work
    102

Beveridge, William 18
Booth, Charles 18
British Association of Social Workers
  (BASW) 121

care *see* children taken into care and
  custody
Child and Adolescent Mental Health
  Service (CAMHS) 35, 38, 111,
  113–15, 118, 119–20, 131, 142
child welfare concerns 25, 33–4, 36–
  7, 39, 65, 74–5, 78–81, 97–8,
  104, 106–7
Children and Young Person's Records
  (CYPRs) 110–11, 114–15,
  118–20
children taken into care and custody
  behaviours, troubled and
    troublesome 100–7, 116–20
  research evidence 107–8
    cohort of children 108–10
    comparison of subgroups
      116–20
    housing tenure, adult issues and
      behaviour 112–14

    profile of need and service
      involvement 110–12,
      113–14
    sequence of service involvement
      114–16
    study discussion and conclusions
      120–2
Coalition Government 12, 20, 53,
  102, 124
'common purpose' approach 7, 9–10
community
  and ASB 13, 62, 120–1
  involving 169–71, 175
  pedagogic approach 176
  responsibility in child protection
    process 164
  in sub-Saharan Africa 162
  violence, countering 168–9
'conscientization' 171, 176
custody *see* children taken into care
  and custody

data protection 45, 105–6, 108
debt 11, 83, 86–7, 103, 133, 177
'dedicated' workers 7, 54, 126
Democratic Republic of the Congo
  (DRC) 169
Denmark 175–6
domestic violence 11, 32, 48, 85,
  103, 133, 155
Dundee Family Project 9, 19, 21

education criterion 43, 45, 47–8, 111
empowering families 171–2
ethic of care 8–9
eugenicist thinking 19
extended family breakdown 160–1

FACIT (Family and Crisis Intervention
    Team) 173–4
Faith's story 35–6
Family Action
    aim 39
    broader impact of services 40–1
    evidence of impact 39–40
    extended funding 31–2
    successes 46
    and TFP Phase 1 32–3
        case studies 33–9
        as TFP provider 30–1
        continuing support 50–2
        TPF provision challenges 41–6
        potential solutions 46–50
family-based/centred services and
    family practice 172–4
Family Group Conferencing (FGC)
    170
Family Intervention Projects (FIPs)
    aims and approach 57–8
    cases
        housing approach 62–7
        social work ethos 58–62
    characteristics 75–6
    comparison with FRP 76, 81,
        96–8, 126
    impetus for 74
    origins 22, 53, 101–2
    policy agenda 17, 20
Family Intervention Worker (FIW) 54,
    55, 56, 66, 68
family preservation programmes 174
Family Recovery Project (FRP)
    case studies 84–7
    casework approaches and methods
        87–91
    characteristics 75–6
    comparison with FIP and TFP
        96–8
    families 78–81, 128–30, 155
        contact with other agencies
            130–2
        views on their difficulties
            132–4

findings
    on effectiveness 92–6, 139–42,
        156–7
    on reaching families 91–2
    rationale 74–5
    research aims and methods 77–8,
        126–8
    service components 81–4
    service continuity 76, 95, 97–8
    team members 76–7
    views on
        of families 134–43
        of other agencies and workers
            143–55
    weaknesses/limitations 147–9,
        152–3, 157
Family Service Units 18, 20
Family Star Plus 40–1, 44–5, 49
Family Support Workers 35–6, 37,
    38, 70
family, terminology of 15–16
Family to Family 175
FIPs see Family Intervention Projects
FRP see Family Recovery Project
funding
    of FRP 128
    pathfinder 74–5
    of TFP 12, 31–2, 43, 51, 97–8

Guatemala 170

HIV/AIDS 163, 165
Home Builders approach 21
housing-related concerns
    assistance prior to FRP 83, 93
    as contribution to poor child
        outcomes 103
    Dundee Family Project 21
    expectations and experiences of
        FRP 134, 138, 139, 142, 154
    Family Action 34, 37
    as family problem 11, 14, 132,
        133
    multi-agencies 177
    Northcity Project 62–7
    as recurring issue 39, 40

ill-health 11, 19, 80, 93
inclusion of families criterion 41–2
intensive family intervention
    family projects 57–8
        Northcity Project 62–7
        Westcity Project 58–62
    introduction to 53–6
    study discussion and conclusion
        67–71
Intensive Outreach Worker (IOW)
    approach of 89
    as bridge-builder 90
    as characteristic of FIPs 75
    as component of FRP 81–2, 84–5,
        86
    role in children's lives 92
    role in TFP 7
    as 'trouble shooter' 14
    see also key workers
international perspectives
    developing appropriate forms of
        social work 162–3
    families
        breakdown of extended 160–1
        countering violence 168–9
        empowering 171–2
        involving 169–71
        listening to 164
        making men responsible for
            164–5
        multi-agencies working for 177
        pedagogic approaches 175–6
        programmes and initiatives
            174–5
        services and practice 172–4
        strengthening 165–6
    introduction to 159–60
    social development
        global agenda for 167–8
        need for role 162
        working towards transformation
            166–7
    study conclusion 178
interventions
    cost of 12–13
    developmental approach 162

FIPs as expansion in family 22
    link to staff skill levels 61, 69
    links with established approaches
        23
    social work 20, 101–2
    TFP 7–10
    see also intensive family intervention

'J' family 84–6
Jamaica 168–9
Jane's story 38–9
Joseph, Keith 18–19, 124
Julie's story 33–4

key workers 7, 54–71
    see also Intensive Outreach Worker
        (IOW)

Latin America 171–2
listening to families 164
local authorities
    children taken into care study
        116–22
    commissioning problems 44
    difficulty in identifying most needy
        families 6, 10, 104–6
    funding provision 12
    key worker training 55
    local inclusion criteria 48
    responsibility for custody
        expenditure 102–3
    Westcity Project 58–62

Maldives 164
Marea Naranja (Orange Wave) 167–8
measurement of success 42–3
mediation skills 90, 135
mental health 33–4, 41–2, 48–9,
    84–6, 103, 131, 163
multi-agencies
    in promoting change 177
    views on FRP 143–54
    working with 45–6

need
 catering for different levels of 43
 indicators of 103, 113–14, 120–1
 profile of 110–12
neo-liberalism 18
Netherlands 177
New Labour Government 13, 19, 53,
  74, 102
New York 173–4
New Zealand 169–71
Northcity Project 62–7
Norway 170

'O' family 86–7
occupational identity
 critical features for intensive family
  project work 57–8
 family intervention key workers
  attitudes, personal qualities and
   working style 54–5
  and social work 68–71
  training 55
 housing approach 62–7
 informal techniques 58
 management of family lifestyles 58
 professional competencies 55–6,
  68–9, 71
 social work ethos approach 58–62
 worker continuity 92

parenting capacity 40, 41–2, 49
Paula's story 36–7
Payment by Results (PBR)
 areas unqualified for 48–9
 contractual end dates 43
 financial risk implications 44
 impact against outcome measures
  39–40
 parents preparing for employment
  97
 reservations about 6, 12–13
 sharing payments between partners
  45–6
 simplification of 50, 51
 suggestions for improvement 46–7
 worklessness 106

Peace Management Institute (PMI)
  168–9
pedagogic approaches 175–6
'persistent, assertive and challenging'
  approach 7, 8–9
policy context 17–20
practical 'hands-on' support 7–8, 39,
  60, 168–9
'problem families' 19, 124–5
professionalism 23–5, 54–6, 58,
  62–4, 66–71, 81–2, 177
progress measures 44–5, 46–7

relational style 24–5
relative poverty 103, 104, 106, 112,
  121
resilience 8–9, 11, 51
risk factors 104–5

safeguarding 25, 80, 96
sanctions 57, 88
school attendance 10, 32, 38–9, 42–
  3, 46, 92–3, 101, 117, 133, 155
service delivery 24–5, 81, 87, 166–7,
  174
'shuttle diplomacy' 90
Signpost 17
single parent families 11, 58, 130,
  134, 139, 155, 168
social work
 developing role in relation to
  troubled families 122
 ethos 24, 58–62, 75
 families with multiple problems
  101–2
 international
  developing appropriate forms of
   162–3
  empowering families 171–2
  family-oriented 159–60, 172–
   4, 178
  global agenda for 167–8
  global definition of 160
  marketisation of 166-7, 177
  need for developmental role
   162

social work *cont.*
  international *cont.*
    working towards transformation
      166–7
  and 'J' family 84–6
  and key workers 68–71
  origins 20–2
  project relations with 65–7
  views on 143
South Africa 166–7
Spain 167–8
special educational needs (SEN) 114,
  116, 119
step-up and step-down services 43
Strengthening Families 170–1
sub-Saharan Africa 162, 164–6
substance misuse 11, 49, 105, 113

Team Around the Family (TAF) 76,
  80, 81–2, 84–5, 94–5, 125, 144
terminology 14–17, 100–1
TFP *see* Troubled Families Programme
Think Family project 7, 75–6, 78–81,
  91
'tough-love' approach 13–14
troubled and troublesome behaviour
  100–7, 116–20
troubled families
  characteristics 10–11
  criteria for 53–4, 103–4
  discontinuity of service 97
  early intervention and prevention
    51
  international concept 159
  limitation of model 157
  perspectives on 125, 172
  prevalence in deprived city areas
    112
  problems with identifying 51,
    97–8, 104–6
  public expenditure 12
  terminology 14–16, 100–1
Troubled Families Programme (TFP)
  aims 92–3, 97, 122
  comparison with FRP 96–8
  criticism 121

eligibility 10–11
focus on behaviour 101
focus on whole family 102, 107
impact
  broader 40–1
  evidence of 39–40
interventions 7–10
  cost of 12–13
  introduction 5–6
  launch 5, 20, 105
  limitations 125
  as non-statutory intervention
    106–7
Phase 1
  challenges in providing 41–6
  criteria for entry 31, 100,
    103–4
  delivering 30–3
Phase 2
  criteria for entry 32
  shaping 46–50
policy context 17–20
practice context 20–3
  professional practice 23–5
rationale 12–14, 100
suggested name change 45
'turning around' 12, 16–17, 53, 125

'underclasses' 18–19
United States
  family-based/centred services and
    family practice 172–4
  family preservation programmes
    174
  Family to Family initiative 175
  influence on social work 171

Vietnam 162–3

Webb, Beatrice and Sidney 18
welfare qualities 13, 18
Westcity Project 58–62, 63, 66
'whole family' approach
  developing theory for 23–4
  for embedded change 52

as feature of FIPs and Think
        Family projects 75
as feature of intensive family
        intervention 57
long tradition of 20–1, 107
relation to TFP 9, 11, 25, 102
tension within 106
worklessness 32, 44, 104, 106
difficulty in finding continuous
        employment 39–40
greater recognition of progress
        towards work 47
worth 13, 15, 169, 173

Zimbabwe 164–6

AUTHOR INDEX

Action for Children 125
Adams, R. 7–8
Alexander, D. 74
Annie E. Casey Foundation, The 175
Askeland, G.A. 160

Batty, E. 54, 64
BBC 125
Blair, T. 125
Boddy, J. 11, 17
Brandon, M. 81
Broadhurst, K. 77

Cabinet Office, Social Exclusion Task
  Force 74
Cameron, A. 70–1
Cameron, C. 176
Cameron, D. 13, 105, 125
Carey, M. 70
Carlsen, M. 166, 176
Casey, L. 11, 14, 24
Children's Workforce Development
  Council (CWDC) 55, 57
Clark, E.J. 173
Collins, D. 173
Conley, A. 166, 175
Connor, S. 18
Conolly, A. 104
Cooper, J. 124
Cox, D. 160–1

Daniel, B. 80–1, 87, 91
Department for Children, Schools and
  Families (DCSF) 74, 78

Department for Communities and
  Local Government (DCLG) 5–13,
  18, 20–3, 24, 48, 54–5, 57,
  107, 125
Department for Education 78
Department of Health 81
Devaney, J. 105
Dillane, J. 9, 11, 19, 21, 125
Dominelli, L. 7–8
Duggan, M. 126

Featherstone, B. 87
Feinstein, L. 104
Felitti, V. 105
Flint, J. 24, 64, 70
Frazer, M.W. 21
Freire, P. 176

Garrett, P.M. 15, 18, 69
Gelles, R.J. 174
Gregg, D. 9, 11, 15, 18, 21, 22, 125

Hall, P. 124
Hatton, K. 175–6
Hayden, C. 10, 11, 13, 17, 24, 25,
  54, 100, 104, 106, 108, 110
Hayes, D. 121
Henderson, M. 170
HM Treasury 74
Hochfeld, T. 166
Holt, A. 104
Howe, D. 7–8
Hoxhallari, L. 104
Hugman, R. 162–3
Hunter, C. 11
Hussain, A. 164

Institute of Public Care (IPC) 103, 104
International Association of Schools of Social Work (IASSW) 167–8
International Council on Social Welfare (ICSW) 167–8
International Federation of Social Workers (IFSW) 164, 167–8

Jenkins, C. 10, 11, 13, 17, 24, 25, 54, 104, 108
Jennisen, T. 173
Jones, D. 167
Jones, R. 10, 17, 67, 69, 71
Joseph, S.D. 126

Kelliher, M. 170
Kendall, S. 75

Laird, S.E. 162
Lawrence, S. 161
Lepper, J. 121
Levitas, R. 12, 15, 104, 125
Levy, H. 168–9
Lloyd, C. 11, 21–2
Lundy, C. 173
Lyon, L. 104
Lyons, J. 166, 176

Macnicol, J. 18
Madge, N. 124
Manion, K. 166, 176
Mason, C. 67, 69
Matthews, R. 69
McKenzie, M. 170
McVeigh, T. 121
Midgley, J. 163, 166, 175
Ministry of Labour, Invalids and Social Affairs (MOLISA) 163
Ministry of Social Affairs 176
Monaghan, A. 121
Morris, K. 8, 11, 14, 15, 16, 23, 87, 108
Moss, P. 176
Murphy, D. 126
Murray, C. 19

National Audit Office 6, 7, 48
National Centre for Social Research (Natcen) 54
Nelson, C.E. 21
Nixon, J. 11, 14, 54–5

Palmer, H. 75
PANOS 165
Parr, S. 10, 11, 13, 16, 17, 18, 21, 24, 25, 63–4, 67, 69, 102, 126
Parsons, C. 104
Patel, L. 166
Pawar, M. 160–1
Payne, M. 7–8, 20, 160
Pickles, E.H.C. 74
Prior, D. 58
Pulitzer Centre 169

Queiro-Tajalli, I. 172

Raniga, T. 167
Rasheed, J.M. 172
Rasheed, M.N. 172
Respect Task Force 13, 19–20, 21, 53
Rivard, J.C. 21
Rodger, J. 75
Rogowski, S. 69
Rotabi, K.S. 170
Ruch, G. 126
Rutter, M. 105, 106, 124

Sabates, R. 104
SAfAIDS 165
Scourfield, P. 70, 71
Seebohm Committee 124
Simpson, G. 18
SOS Children's Villages 165–6
Spratt, T. 101, 102, 104, 105
Squires, P. 102
Starkey, P. 19, 20
Stenson, K. 58

Talbot, C. 125
Thoburn, J. 7, 10, 11, 12, 14, 18, 20, 24, 25, 74, 78, 80, 81, 87, 97, 107, 125

Thompson, N. 14
Truell, R. 167
Turner, F. 126

UNAIDS 165
UNICEF Vietnam 162–3

Van der Laan, G. 177
Van Ewijk, H. 176

Watkins, J. 173
Welshman, J. 18, 19
White, C. 11, 19, 54–5
White, S. 87, 97
Williams, F. 8, 16
Wincup, E. 12, 15–16
Woodhouse, C. 14
Woods-Waller, G. 173

York Consulting 75, 91

Zelnick, J. 167